HOW TO DO THINGS RIGHT

How To Do Things Right

THE REVELATIONS OF A FUSSY MAN

by L. RUST HILLS

Doubleday & Company, Inc., Garden City, New York 1972

Grateful acknowledgment is made to the magazines in which these essays first appeared.

"How and When Properly to Make and Eat Milk Toast" first appeared in *McCall's Magazine.* © 1972 L. Rust Hills.

"How to Organize a Family Picnic (and Keep It That Way)" first appeared in *Audience* magazine. © 1971 Hill Publishing Company.

"How to Eat an Ice-Cream Cone" first appeared in *The New Yorker.* © 1968 The New Yorker Magazine, Inc.

"How to Cut Down on Smoking and Drinking Quite So Much" first appeared in *Audience* magazine. © 1972 Hill Publishing Company.

"How to Do Four Dumb Tricks with a Package of Camels" first appeared in *Esquire* magazine. © 1969 by L. Rust Hills.

"How to Solve America" first appeared in *Harper's Magazine.* © 1972 by The Minneapolis Star-Tribune Co., Inc.

"Delight in Order" first appeared in *Audience* magazine. © 1971 Hill Publishing Company.

FOR PENNEY—
WHO ENCOURAGED ME TO DO THIS
SO EVERYBODY WOULD KNOW
WHAT SHE HAS HAD TO PUT UP WITH.

Contents

vii

Publisher's Note

Orderly people all over the world will be heartened to learn that this is but the first book in a projected Fussy Man trilogy. *HOW TO DO THINGS RIGHT: The Revelations of a Fussy Man* will be followed in the course of things by *HOW TO RETIRE AT FORTY-ONE, or Life Among the Routines and Pursuits and Other Problems,* in which the author tells how he quit work in the prime of life so as to contend full-time with the minutiae of day-to-day living. This will be followed, by the magnum opus, *HOW TO BE GOOD, or The Somewhat Tricky Business of Attaining Moral Virtue in a Society That's Not Just Corrupt but Corrupting, Without Being Completely Out-of-It.*

Introductory Note

If you are interested in doing something right (for a change), my revelations will surely help you. You'll find all the answers here, no matter what the question that is bothering you: whether it be how to save your marriage, what to do about America's industrial growth, how you can be absolutely certain your alarm will go off in the morning, or how to counteract the chaos and immorality of modern life. All the answers to such specific questions (and many, many more) are given on a step-by-step basis. And the principles by which you can solve virtually any other question are clearly set forth.

Now it may seem to some of you as you first get into this that the answers are harder than the questions, that the solutions in fact turn out to be far worse than the problems ever even thought of being. But that's because you don't yet understand the problems-and-solutions relationship. Anyone interested in doing something right, *really right,* is necessarily going to be much more intrigued by a problem than he is by a solution. If you are only interested in a solution—just any old simple solution —then the best thing to do is not even *think* about the problem. Most problems just go away—*poof!*—if you stop thinking about them.

Difference in degree of interest-in-the-problem creates the fundamental division of all mankind: between those who believe in *getting things done,* on the one hand, and those who believe in *doing things right,* on the other. Most of the complex problems we've got in this country today are the result of slap-dash, "can-do" men attempting to solve once-simple problems in careless ways that left a mess, left vicious half-solved problems, like wounded lions, in all our streets. Simple solutions and easy ways seem very seductive, but when you go to repair something for the third or fourth time you realize it would have been truly easier to have done the job carefully in the first place. "The right way is the hard way" sounds like an LCT (one of Life's Cruel Truths), but a reasonable man wouldn't have it otherwise. For the hard way to be the wrong way too would be completely unfair; it's bad enough the way it is.

Say the newsmen are asking the press secretary about a specific problem. "Oh yes," he assures them, "we're doing something about that." What "something" means here is *any*thing, for the emphasis is really on the *doing;* and whatever it is they're doing will eventually shape their conception of what the problem was. The solution will determine the problem, instead of the right way around. How much better if the spokesman were to say: "We're becoming fascinated by that problem, as a matter of fact, and we're watching it develop so as to determine the steps necessary to solve it forever."

Problems have their pride, you know, as well as a strong sense of self-preservation, and they quite naturally resist yielding up their existence to an inferior solution. But when a problem is confronted with a solution that demonstrates full appreciation and entire comprehension—matches it intricacy for intricacy, complexity for complexity, even absurdity for absurdity—then it gives way utterly to this flattery and understanding. A completely solved problem is as beautiful and untroublesome as a completely satisfied woman—and just as rare, of course, especially these days.

Since the "perfect" solution to a problem, the *exact* match-up, is unlikely to occur to anyone, a certain amount of overkill in problem-solving is not just necessary but quite obviously necessary. Thus what I present in this book (proudly) is a sequence of apparently complicated solutions to apparently simple problems. The fact that they may not work either is completely irrelevant. It's *a whole new approach!* It shows that what we must do to make our problems succumb to us is first comprehend them, then appreciate them, and finally actually delight in them.

So, as the First Revelation of the Fussy Man, I say unto you, verily: Learn to *love* thy problems as thy self.

Who is this Fussy Man anyway, you ask, and where does he get all these Revelations? I wonder about that too, and I've been considering just what's the relation of my own puny self to the giant know-it-all figure who stalks these pages, the Fussy Man, telling everyone how to do everything right.

Is that *me* peering into the broiler to make sure my toast is done just right? I guess I maybe have done that. I may also have organized a family picnic or two in my time, but I certainly never made the family get out of the car to show what they could carry—although we did have countdowns, God knows. There *is* a sign that says "Cleaning up as you go along is half the fun" over the kitchen sink, but not *all* those signs are around the house, not yet anyway. You see how it goes; it's like watching home movies in which you appear: You can't deny it's you, but you sort of wish it weren't. Maybe you were just putting on an act for the camera.

I have to admit we have a lot in common, though, the Fussy Man and I. We both seem to own twenty far-from-trouble-free acres on the Connecticut coast way the hell-and-gone up near Rhode Island. We both seem to have a wife and stepchildren who are sometimes around and sometimes not. We both seem somehow *different* from time to time (hard to explain). We both seem somewhat underemployed (out of work) and yet overoccupied (busy, busy). And we both seem subject to fits of lassitude and despair. Since we both seem to know so well how things *should* be done: How come things don't actually *do* right for us?

In our paranoid moods (i.e., most of the time these days), the Fussy Man and I feel that all these Revelations about How to Do Things Right were maybe sent to us as another of God's jokes, like the one He kept playing on Moses. You remember how He sent down The Ten Commandments and then made the Israelites keep forgetting them; then He'd get after Moses about it, and Moses would tighten the people up for a while; then they'd start forgetting again. The Commandments are pretty good rules, easy to understand; and ten is a nice round number, too, scarcely harder to remember than the five things you have to do to set an alarm clock. How come people can't do a few simple things like that, the way they ought to?

The answer, of course, is that human life is by nature chaotic and that any attempt to impose order on it is as absurd as Hitler's mustache. That's the *answer*. But as I've said, questions are far more intriguing than answers. The fun in it all is acting *as if* human problems could be solved—if there is in fact any fun in it, which I'm beginning more and more to think there isn't, not anywhere near as much as I thought anyway.

Still, what are the alternatives?

The irony is, that within this admittedly essential wrongness that's implicit in any futility, we *are* right, the Fussy Man, God, Moses, and me. Things *would* be better if people did things right. The trouble is that the sloppy people just go ahead and get things done, in their half-assed way, then take strength from that and go on and do something else, while we fussy people hang around deploring all the mess. I believe (and common sense demands you do too) that seven eighths of what's done nowadays is not just not worth doing but would be better off left *un*done. It's clear to me, therefore, that the fussy, ineffective person who does practically nothing, but does it right, stands in a State of Grace substantially higher than all those others who do a lot of things badly. But *they're* the ones who get to do it all! The poor tidy fellow who believes "No job is ever done until the tools are put away" keeps finding he has to clean up the workbench first, before he can even start. So he's standing there in his State of Grace, doing a slow burn.

Thus it cometh about that many fussy people are either pretty angry or very lonely, and sometimes both. It appears we are more cursed than blessed by our rage for order. An orderly person is usually either feared or laughed at. And since to be feared is surely the worst thing there is, I come to my Second Revelation: We must study harder to be laughed at.

L. Rust Hills

HOW TO DO THINGS RIGHT

PART ONE

Delight in Order

"It is beautiful to see the footgear ranged in a row according to its kind; beautiful to see garments sorted according to their use, and coverlets; beautiful to see glass vases and tableware so sorted; and beautiful, too, despite the jeers of the witless and flippant, to see cooking-pots arranged with sense and symmetry. Yes, all things without exception, because of symmetry, will appear more beautiful when placed in order. All these utensils will then seem to form a choir; the center which they unite to form will create a beauty that will be enhanced by the distance of the other objects in the group."

—XENOPHON
Economics

❊ *Delight in Order*

THE ONLY NIETZSCHE I EVER READ WAS IN MARCH 1969 ON one of those temporary boardings around a construction site, 52nd and 5th, NE corner, NYC, as follows:

> "ONE MUST HAVE CHAOS IN ONE
> TO GIVE BIRTH TO A DANCING STAR"
> —NIETZCHE

Carefully, *tidily* written it was, in (this seemed significant) *magic* marker, there in all the chaos of that corner, with the air compressors going and all. The building that's since gone up at 52nd, and 5th, NE corner, is proof enough, if anyone needed it, that chaos doesn't necessarily produce a dancing star. Must one really have chaos *in him* to give birth to a dancing star? Who wants to give birth to a dancing star anyway? I mean, maybe the mothers of Nijinsky and Cyd Charisse or whatever her name was do, but who else? And what I really want

5

to know is this: How come whoever wrote that Nietzsche quote there, if he believed so in chaos, printed it out so neatly, even if he did misspell the man's name?

Against that saying of Nietzsche's I'd any day put one or another of my own. There's for instance the one that, one Christmas, my stepdaughter painted for me, in a messy but still kind of beautiful way, red and brown oil color on board, now installed over our kitchen sink, the most appropriate place, inscribing more or less permanently one of my most oft-iterated and deeply-held convictions:

> CLEANING UP AS YOU GO ALONG
> IS HALF THE FUN

Then on a sort of sill-board under it is another; I did this carefully in magic marker myself, and it doesn't look half so nice:

> ONE OF LIFE'S GREATEST PLEASURES
> IS PUTTING SOMETHING BACK WHERE IT BELONGS

Our kitchen's beginning to look like Montaigne's famous tower room, where he had quotations from his favorite classic authors painted all around the walls—except all ours has is just the collected wit and wisdom of L. Rust Hills. "My Admonishments" I'd call them, except I like "My Admonitions" too and can't choose between the words.

What I think would be nice to have next is a lovingly

designed, carefully embroidered sampler to hang over our eating table, again the most appropriate place. It would say:

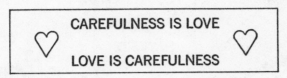

CAREFULNESS IS LOVE

LOVE IS CAREFULNESS

Then I could simply point up at it reproachfully when someone spilled, or if I were served a brusquely-prepared meal. A woman in love with a man doesn't serve him lamb that's either overdone or underdone; she takes care to do it right. Children who love their parents (remember them?) take care never to spill or slop or speak with their mouths full. Tidy rooms and a clean kitchen show a loving, careful spirit. Everyone moves slowly and carefully when love is in the air, especially carefully.

There's a whole psychology that claims the opposite is true: that the careful, tidy person is anal, authoritarian, rigid, irascible, and unloving. We fussy people know how false this is; we know how much love is locked in our hearts, waiting for others to be careful enough to deserve it. We in fact watch the others constantly, looking for the sort of carefulness we could give our love to. And all they (the others) say is that our watching them that way makes them nervous and that's half the reason they spill. The world's psychologies and philosophies are full of justifications for the sloppy, the careless, the accident-prone—while we fussy are left without defense. Never mind—perhaps we can have another sign made, appropriate, I'd say (or admit), this time for the bathroom, that would provide us some solace:

> FUSSINESS
> IS ITS OWN
> REWARD

For the ultimate sign, after I've flipped completely, I'm going to the zoning board and ask for a variance so that I can install a giant neon sign on the roof, one that flashes on and off, with a twin message to the world. First it would say:

> DISORDER IS THE ULTIMATE EVIL

Then that would blink off and this would flash on:

> ORDER IS THE INITIAL GOOD

And they'd alternate that way, all through the night, lightening the dark, spreading truth throughout the land.

Notice that we're speaking of disorder as the *ultimate* evil, while all we claim for order is that it is the *initial* good. No one would claim order as any kind of ultimate virtue; it's probably the most boring of the virtues, and they're all pretty boring. But just as disorder is the product or result or effect of all the vices, so order is the beginning or source or cause of all the virtues. Take a vice like sloth, it leads to disorder, so does adultery, they all do. The beds never get made: where Vice reigns,

8

Mess stands close beside the throne. On the other hand, the virtues all flourish in an orderly environment. "Good order is the foundation of all good things," said Edmund Burke, in *Reflections on the Revolution in France*, according to my *Stevenson's Quotations*. I just mention this in case you put more stock in what Edmund Burke says than in what I tell you.

The thing about both order and disorder is that they spread. Disorder, as is well known (i.e., a cliché), spreads like wildfire—that is, I suppose, much too fast and out of control. But order spreads too—not far, not fast, not like wildfire certainly, but it still spreads. How order spreads is in an orderly way: slowly, calmingly, carefully, even neatly. But the key thing about how order spreads is that it spreads from the inside out. Order, to be natural, good, real order, must begin within.

Any kind of inflicted order, order imposed from the outside in, or from the top down, to try to straighten anything out, only makes the mess worse in the long run. Imposed order is worse than no order. You can't run a household by posting a lot of rules. If a nation is controlled by a repressive regime, it is an indication the society is disorderly, not orderly. Order need not, indeed ought not, be hierarchical—we've had all that in the social structures of the past, and the people on the bottom didn't like it as much as the people on the top and because there were more of them, this misorder created disorder.

Rules, regulations, forms, controls—all such aspects of a managed and manipulated society—aren't at all the kind of order I'm trying to praise. Nor, for God's sake, do I mean order as in the dreadful pro-police catch

9

phrase "law and order." Any kind of New Order, national or otherwise, that sets out to straighten the world by ruling it, is hateful, disruptive, intolerable totalitarianism. And any kind of New Order that seeks to regulate even without ruling is appalling, intolerable creeping bureaucracy. None of these is the kind of order one can delight in. These are all aspects of an unnatural order imposed by the state on the individual, instead of the natural order of composed and balanced individuals and functioning institutions contributing order to the state. One wants to regulate his own life, not have it done for him.

If you get yourself straightened out and settled down, it's going to help your wife get herself in order too; it's bound to. And this in turn will have a good effect on the kids. Maybe even the dog will get less yappy and nervous, and that will please the neighbors. Order spreads slowly, but it spreads. Real order, the order which is worth seeking, begins with the composed, balanced, secure individual; spreads (one hopes) through the composed, balanced, secure family; extends (perhaps) to the composed, balanced, secure community; and thence (with the participation of millions) to the nation; and from there (triumphantly) to an ordered, composed, balanced (and grateful) world. But you have to start with yourself—you first, then your wife and kids, and only after the dog do you tackle the Town Hall.

Take a thing like meals on time—breakfast, lunch, and dinner all served at more or less exactly the same time each day, every day of the week, except Sunday, which has its own regular but different schedule. Meals on time can provide a good rigid basic structure to the day plan and can be a great force for order in one's life. Questions like "What time do you think you'll decide you want dinner?" (from one's wife) or "Hasn't dinner even been started yet?" (from the kids) require careful handling during the period of preprandial irascibility. Kids like to know exactly when dinner is. In fact, everyone in the family likes the idea of meals being at a regular, old-fashioned, definite time. That's not to say it isn't harder than hell and maybe even impossible to arrange with a wife who isn't a servant and kids who aren't just house-guests with no plans of their own. But the main thing in setting out to establish this sort of order in your life and your family's life is to have yourself under control, so that if you do manage to set up a regular system of mealtimes, you yourself are always ready to eat the meal at the time specified, not just when you feel like it. You can't skip coming to the luncheon table because you aren't hungry, and you can't delay dinner a half hour while you have a second whiskey sour. It all starts with you.

Doing something, more or less anything, *regularly*, helps to establish order. But it should be an order that pleases you. A swim before lunch, walking home from work on good days, playing squash twice a week in the winter and tennis in the summer, bridge with the couple next door Wednesday nights, getting drunk every Friday, going to church every Sunday, paying the bills the tenth of every month—all such patterns of behavior, if they help you like your life, should be developed. If they cause you trouble or if they bore you, then forget them and find others that you do like. And don't let it all get too involved, these schedules and routines: the idea of ordering your life is to simplify it, not complicate it further. The ordered life has pattern and texture; but the pattern should be simple and pleasing and of your own design, and the texture should be loose and comfortable—the whole garment made to order and to fit, but especially to *order*. If homespun is spun too rough or tight, one gets to feeling all confined and hot and scratchy and breaks out. That's no good.

On the refrigerator, a great big good old solid GE monitor-top made God knows when, the kind my father used to sell when he worked for Rex Cole, who used to be sole distributor for General Electric products in the New York City area and you can imagine how long ago that was—on this refrigerator, which is the one thing we have that never seems to break down (touch wood), and the reason it never breaks down, I swear, is because it was made so long ago it doesn't realize it's entitled to —anyway, *on* this refrigerator, it says:

ONLY THE BORED WELCOME THE UNEXPECTED

---

another of my admonishments, one that now seems to me to cut two ways.

Originally I composed it to refute the absurd position, taken by some in the household, that it's nicer not to be told in advance what's for dinner but to wait and be surprised. "Surprises," as I've always understood them, are substantially different from just not knowing what to expect. Surprises are—or used to be when I was a deserving little lad—something "special" or "extra," anyway, *good*. But now when they won't tell you what they're having for dinner, it's not because it's so good or extra or special; they're just trying to postpone the "Oh, not again" reaction for as long as they can. The whole concept of "a nasty surprise," as in the sentence, "*He sure got a nasty surprise*," has always seemed something of a contradiction in terms to me—but then so, too, I admit, does the concept of "an unexpected pleasure."

"What's for dessert?" you ask halfway through dinner, wondering whether or not to have seconds, trying to eat your dinner *right*, to achieve that delicate balance between fulfillment and desire.

"Wait-and-see pudding," they say to you, cheerfully, maddeningly.

What "wait-and-see pudding" *means*, of course, is that there *isn't* anything planned for dessert. One ends up having "S, B, and C" (sliced bananas and cream) or vanilla ice cream from the freezer with shavings of German's semisweet chocolate on top. Both are delicious, I admit. But they're not as good (except once in a while) as what we call a "made" dessert that someone's planned ahead, even though it may not have come out too well.

"ONLY THE BORED WELCOME THE UNEXPECTED" attempts to influence not just the refrigerator but also the calendar, which is stuck to the side of the refrigerator with magnets. Originally, again, it was an effort to persuade householders to mark on the calendar in advance any invitations extended or accepted, so that fewer comings and goings would occur unexpectedly. But it doesn't seem as apt to me as it once did. One is sometimes bored enough to welcome *anyone* who drives in—unexpected or not—that's true. But when you're really *really* bored you enjoy anticipating a major event like going out to dinner, want to know about it as far in advance as possible, and rather lament the waste involved when someone asks you at the last minute.

This suggests my admonition's other edge. It seems to me now that it takes basic order (boredom in this case, but there's more to it) to delight in disorder (the unexpected, but more there too). The sign over our boathouse workbench:

DELIGHT IN ORDER

of course plays off Robert Herrick's famous poem:

DELIGHT IN DISORDER
A sweet disorder in the dress
Kindles in clothes a wantonness:
A lawn about the shoulders thrown
Into a fine distraction:
An erring lace, which here and there
Enthralls the crimson stomacher;
A cuff neglectful, and thereby
Ribbands to flow confusedly;
A winning wave (deserving note)
In the tempestuous petticoat;
A careless shoe-string, in whose tie
I see a wild civility:
Do more bewitch me than when art
Is too precise in every part.

Now I know that as a somewhat sloppy person you've always been very fond of this poem, and I'll have to admit it's real good: all the slippery, sloppy, slithery S-sounds, as if sexy, silken slip-straps were ceaselessly sliding off seductive shoulders all over the place; and the fluid liquidity of it, especially in such lines as "whenas in silks my Julia goes" and "that liquefaction of her clothes"; and the functionally irregular and disordered stresses leading up to the precisely iambed couplet—

> Do more bewitch me than when art
> Is too precise in every part

—parodying by epitomizing the very perfection it mocks; all these sounds, and more, enhance the sense superbly. But now just what in fact is it you're saying the sense of the poem is? What is its meaning in this order-disorder argument? Does the poem set forth a theory of art—extolling some loose "natural" Romantic or Gothic notion of art over the refinements and internal unities and harmonies of the Classical and Neoclassical art that are too precise in every part? Or is it a statement on laws and ethics? Or maybe it's just a kind of lecherous lyric? The idea is there, surely, that a woman who is a little careless in her dress may be a little careless with her virtue—which is what I think of as the messy-is-sexy fallacy.

But notice how qualified what Herrick says is. He speaks of "a *sweet* disorder," "a *fine* distraction," "*an* erring lace" (i.e., *one*, not the whole bunch), and a "civility" that may be "wild," but is still *civility*. I think all you've got here is the poet saying that so long as there's a good basic order it's kind of nice and exciting sometimes in a strange way to have a *little* disorder. No one's going to deny that.

In fact, I wish it said it over the inside of our front door, so we'd all see it on our way out:

ORDER IS THE MOTHER OF FREEDOM

15

You can't believe how liberating order can be, or could be, if it ever were achieved. I once spent four hours making a list of 183 things to have for dinner, so my wife wouldn't have to plan menus more than twice each year. She claimed she lost the list, and you can't help that, but that's the kind of potential labor-saving, decision-eliminating ordering and planning that *could* produce freedom of mind and time. Oh, an ordered household is much less work and worry! You don't have to fret so much about when to do something or the best way; you just do it how and when you always do it. You don't even have that awful worry about what you ought to do next; just do whatever it is you usually do then, that time of day, that day of the week, that time of the year. Having fewer options to reject may not sound like freedom on the face of it, but in our option-ridden, option-*burdened* society, it is, it is.

And if boredom with routine ever sets in—and while I'm not enough of an optimist to believe that a regular household routine could ever really be established these days, I'm still enough of a pessimist to realize that Restlessness would move right in behind it—then you can (or could) do something else, perfectly certain that you do in fact *want* to do it, and secure that your household, your family, and your own real life will still run along in its well-run way.

I say this because I know, for instance, that you've still got in your mind's eye that delightfully disordered lady we saw downtown, the one whose clothes were always slipping and sliding. Undoubtedly there's a reason you're attracted to this sort of person. I can't say I exactly approve, but the freedom to do that sort of thing comes with the ordered life too. The Victorians *knew* all this, for God's sake; we just forgot it. So, as long as everything's straightened out at home (made your bed? tidied your room? paid the bills?), well, then, if you *do* want to indulge in what you vulgarly refer to as "a little hanky-panky" or what I describe with infinitely more delicacy as "a consummated flirtation," you can go ahead and do it now and then, naughty person, secure that your own basic life is on rails, so to speak, proceeding in your absence in its orderly, if slightly hypocritical, way.

This sort of genteel excursion, which doesn't disrupt your life or anyone else's, is entirely different from the appalling promiscuity and deplorable philandering that is so compulsive and common among the depraved women and dissolute men of the nasty urban centers these sinful days. That's a kind of moral disorder that shapes their whole lives—or *fails* to shape them, really, for a life of lechery is a life abandoned, you know that. In their case, a sad sordid sequence of "love affairs," so-called, becomes like the point of life, and of course causes great mess and misery. But in an ordered life an occasional cheerful well-planned liaison disrupts nothing: basically pleased with your regulated life, you return to it happily. Q.E.D.: Order is the mother of Freedom.

I don't know how the people you know live, but how most everyone I know lives is in the city, with a house in the country, two or more kids, two cats and/or one dog, a live-in Dutch girl or West Indian babysitter, a two-day-a-week cleaning lady, a once-a-week laundry lady, and arrangements for extra babysitters for Sundays and for Wednesdays when the Dutch girl goes to her English class and for the other nights when she goes out with her boy friend, which is happening more and more often and is not just a nuisance but a worry because the boy friend is a slick guy with no job and gives her a hard time. The wife works part-time; the husband works *all* the time. There just can't possibly *be* any more complicated way to live than this—I've lived more or less that way myself, and I know. The house in the country requires having at least two of everything (everything!) or else jackassing everything back and forth every Friday and Sunday night in the Volvo station-wagon or VW bus. Someone someday will write a great epic poem about these heroic people—cataloging their possessions, celebrating the complexity of their arrangements, chronicling their comings and goings—some Homer of Manhattan's East Nineties. Or perhaps a Sophocles is needed, or an Allen Ginsberg, to show the finest minds of our generation in despair, deranged by the Home Management Muddle.

Most of the people I know seem to be getting divorces now. And of course it's no wonder. One or the other in each couple is insisting on what he or she calls "a chance for a new life before it's too late." Who can blame them? Not even the person they're married to blames them much: "Yeah, well," the other one says, "I wouldn't mind a new life myself." And they add to this, when you have lunch with them separately: "I want to begin over, *more simply.*"

But then they go through a period of even greater complexity and disorder and unhappiness when the complications of the divorce are added to the complications of their regular life. Divorcing husbands gypsy around town gratefully moving into the apartments of friends who are away for two weeks or maybe even just a weekend, promising to water the plants but forgetting to. Predatory nomads they are, but vulnerable too. Divorcing wives try to take up "dating" again at age thirty-five and go out with their dentist's bachelor brother—and lay him, most likely, and then are ashamed to go to their next dental appointment. The children spend the week with the mother, the weekend with the father, and the arrangements by which they are "dropped off" and "picked up" are so intricate and precise that they require a good will and cooperation the parents may not have shown one another for years.

And some of the people I know, after suffering through this (and, of course, much much more) have actually come out the other side and really managed to "begin a new life." And it usually *is* simpler, *much* simpler in fact. They find someone else of course, although they always say they aren't interested in that; but it's seldom the sex-boat their divorcing spouse thinks is what they wanted. Sex is seldom the real problem in these marriages, I'm pretty sure, although who can tell? They're bored with each other, probably—sexually as well as otherwise—but there's enough sex around these days for anyone who isn't either hopelessly timid or utterly insatiable. I'm convinced that what people now divorce to get, besides "a simpler life," is companionship.

Why else do so many divorced men and women marry people they work with? They want someone who knows what they're doing—and without a lot of explanation. A man catches the last train to Greenwich after the most fantastic day at the office—two disasters averted and three crucial deadlines met—gets home about ten or eleven, and his wife, who's sore he missed dinner again and exhausted from *her* day, tries to be cheerful, smiles somewhat falsely, and asks: "Well, what'd you do today?" How can he begin to explain? Suburban housewives are like hopelessly out of the picture, and they know it and are always trying to move back "in." But that doesn't do them any good: they end up spending the summer in Vermont somewhere, two and a half months alone with the kids. "Nice and cool up there too, where she is," the husband says to his assistant as they enter an air-conditioned bar, and she has to make it up to him—the assistant, that is.

The divorcing husband signs everything over to his wife ("Everything!" as he complains later. *"Everything! I was a fool! I just had to get out!"*) and either buries himself in his work or suddenly abandons it altogether and, with his new companion to help, turns to what he "really" wants to do, what he really wanted to do "all along."

And they do live simply, these two—not just because of the alimony, but by preference as well—in a small austerely furnished apartment or someone else's fully furnished home. They're inseparable, do everything together: they even run errands together by choice, instead of saving time by doing things separately. There's plenty of time now: no children, no Home Management Muddle. The old life was complicated but not companionable; the new life is simple but not lonely. And the work gets done: she helps him, or they each have their jobs and meet for drinks right after work and compare notes and know all about what the other's doing. Movies together, weekends alone together, vacations together, work to-gether. They flirt with the idea of buying or building a home, and say they "dream" of it; but they go on renting as long as they can. Sometimes one or the other even balks at marrying: "We're so happy the way we are now," he explains, "I'm afraid that marriage would somehow spoil it." What they mean by that is that they don't want their lives to get so complicated again—with children, households, "things"—that trying to manage it all will separate them.

There's undoubtedly an immaturity to these "new lives," to these "companionate marriages"—a kind of babes clinging together in the wilderness about it, and perhaps some refusal to accept the parental role, although this is certainly not always the case. But the thing is, Man and Woman have always gotten along best when working together, "side by side," from the Garden of Eden to homesteading on the American Frontier, and it is somehow tragic (as well, of course, as comic) that the division of labor required simply to cope with complexity of modern (urbanized, bureaucratized, industrialized) life so often drives them apart.

I've nothing against divorce, God knows. It's the un-happiness that causes the divorce that I find hateful. And what causes this unhappiness is the inability to cope, the impossibility of keeping "on top" of all the things that keep popping up, the sad inadequacy of our efforts to keep together in our lives and to keep our lives together. And what causes this inability to cope, this disorder, is the complexity of the way we attempt to live.

What we middle-class people want or need or yearn for and try to establish is something to resemble the Old

Order, the kind of order our parents, or if not them then our grandparents, used to be able to maintain in their homes, whether they had less or more money than we do now. We want something of the old, less chaotic, more structured world of value-oriented, careful, mannerly behavior, where things made sense, and there was time to read. This kind of Old Order is simply not available to us—the chaos and complexity and tempo of modern life flatly disallow it. The rich can, or could if they wished, perhaps achieve something like the old middle-class order now, could isolate themselves from the chaos and complexity if they chose, could slow life down to something like the old pace. But we want all the accouterments of the rich—the house in the country, the apartment in town, or the big suburban house and grounds, the private schools, or the five-acre zoned-residential area in a good school district, the clothes from Brooks or Bergdorf's, the two cars, one a sports car, the vacations in foreign lands —without having anything like the kind of back-up money not just to pay for them but to maintain them. These poor, very-well-paid (but heavily taxed) professional or business people *have* all these things, but they haven't either the extra money to hire, or the experience to train, competent people to manage and carry for them. The Dutch girl and the West Indian babysitter, with their boyfriends and their language difficulties and long conversations and sudden worrisome overnight absences —they sometimes seem to take up more time than they save. Most of these professional people are too liberal, or too kind, to exploit servants: they don't "handle" them "right." And there's no real room for servants either, in the apartment, the summer house, and the VW bus:

privacy's at a premium in modern life, for both master and man, mistress and maid. And there's no real reason anyway, now I think of it and you're talking that snooty way about "man and master," that somebody else should break his ass just so *you* can try to live the elegant life like your grandfather.

It should be clear, then, that it's necessary to simplify our lives before we'll be *able* to order them.

On the inside of one cupboard door, it says:

> SIMPLIFY. SIMPLIFY. SIMPLIFY.

but inside the cupboard itself is an extraordinary disarrangement of mixing bowls and baking dishes. There seems to be no way to keep these in neat piles, a smaller one nestled cozily inside a larger, the whole pile taking no more room than the largest bowl itself. Some of the baking dishes are square, some rectangular, some are round pie plates, some Mexican, some Pyrex. The bowls are not a set, but an assortment: nice old pale-brown bowls that we like. They don't fit with one another and there are too many of them anyway, far more than are ever needed or used. None of our coffee cups and saucers match either, but they too are sort of old, and we like them.

What I'm getting at at the moment is not another of my admonishments, but one of my LCT's. Surely it is one of Life's Cruel Truths that "things are nicest just before they wear out." This is true of all clothes—of soft khaki trousers and faded blue jeans, old frayed neckties and favorite jackets with leather patches and torn linings. It's true of wooden boats and frame houses and beloved old green convertibles. It is not necessarily true of marriages, of course; but I'm talking about *things* at the moment.

The ramshackle is a falsely simple stage: difficult to achieve and even harder to maintain. It's said of the things I build—floats and porches and bookcases and kindling boxes and so on—that they look old as soon as they are finished. That's because I thriftily use wood that was once something else, so it's battered and somewhat warped just to begin with. The driveway as I like it has grass growing through the gravel—it's just at the point where you really ought to do something about it or you're in for a lot of work later. A rickety pier is what we all love to look at and to feel its silvery weathered wood —but we know next winter's ice will take it out. The ramshackle is lovely to some of us—not because it's functional, but despite the fact it isn't; not because it's fragile, but despite the fact it is. Despite *ourselves* is how some of us like the ramshackle, *despite* our rage for order.

> A lawn about the driveway grown
> Into a fine distraction . . .

These are aesthetic indulgences that the ordered life permits, or ought to. Order is an aspect not of compulsion but of tranquillity, or should be.

When my wife cleans out the refrigerator from time to time, I never fail to tell her: an icebox should never *need* to be cleaned. Just don't ever put anything dirty *into* it, just keep track of what's in there, *use* it regularly and systematically, and you'll never have to clean it out or ever throw anything away. If I lived alone, I'd never have to clean out the icebox, I know. I'd never put anything in unless I had the *definite intention* of taking it out and eating it soon, or fairly soon. Defrost now and then I might have to, yes; but clean it out, never.

But is there anything sadder in the world to contemplate than a big old GE monitor-top used solely by one fussy man? Instead of bursting with stuff—God knows what it all is!—the way it is now, there'd just be a few jars, tidy and righteous and lonely, in one corner. No good. A fussy man needs something to be fussy *about*. We wouldn't like it living alone, my admonishments and me.

There are, then, also emotional considerations that the ordered life takes into account, or ought to. Again: Order is an aspect not of compulsion but of tranquillity, or should be. It's an approach to life, not the absence of life.

What I mean by order, when I'm being serious, is not neatness and tidiness and cleanliness—not the every-chair-in-place, polished-ashtrays, never-an-open-book-left-lying, so-called but misnamed "living" rooms of upper-middle-class suburbs of medium-sized Midwestern cities; there's no beauty there, nor life either; everyone's down in the cellar in the pseudo-pine-paneled, also misnamed, "play" room, watching TV.

What I do mean by order is not taking on more than you can manage without still being able to do what you "really" want. What order is, is not purchasing a lot more stuff than you can fairly easily pay for—not because debts are "bad" as such, but because they end up worrying you and because you don't really need the stuff anyway and you have to maintain it and lug it around with you and get it fixed when it breaks. Order is the opposite of complicating; it's simplifying. Order is not getting deeply entangled with another woman, so you don't get her problems on top of your own. Order is like not wasting a lot of time trying to find things. Order's avoiding a lot of recriminations because you didn't do something you said you would; and maybe it's not saying you'll do a lot of things to begin with. Order is scrupulousness and meticulousness in arrangements with others, so neither of you gets screwed. It's doing things right, or fairly right. It's establishing so far as possible a sense of a regular, regulated, on-going household, so the family can come and go in freedom, knowing there's definitely a place to come back to and what it'll be like when they get there, get home. Order's in like not having to worry too much that you've forgotten something again. Basically what order is, is not getting in over your head.

Order is definitely not things like regimentation and repression. Order's freedom, or at least freeing. One last time: Order's not an aspect of compulsion, but of tranquillity—the tranquillity that permits you to do what you really want.

The trouble is, the disorder in our lives accumulates so gradually that by the time it bugs us it seems too late to do anything about it and we're not sure we want to anyway. This is especially so in our married lives, but is true of other aspects too, our business and general busyness. The growing complexity seems a natural part of growing older and assuming responsibility. Children, promotions, possessions, are in fact all very much wanted when they arrive. A lot of the "things" we own—the extra car, the summer house, the children's TV—are acquired in the delusion that they will make things "better" and (especially ironic) "easier." They ultimately do not, of course, because most of these "conveniences" do not simplify but further complicate. Disappointment leads to dissatisfaction which leads to disillusionment which leads to something quite like desperation and despair. It all gets to be too *much*. One is in over one's head and simply must get out.

At that point we are especially susceptible to the secret message of the media—our Only Provider of values and guidance—the hidden message they've all along been selling you things you didn't need with:

1. Buy something with *sex* (say, a car);
2. Buy something with *youth* (say, gasoline);
3. Buy *escape* (say, a pay-later vacation).

And the companion? Don't think the media's not onto what you call your "essential loneliness." What hidden motivation do you think "Me and my Winstons, we got a real good thing" is probing at, if it isn't your childish companionship need? Sure, go ahead:

4. Buy *companionship* (say, cigarettes and beer).

But it doesn't *do* it, does it? The products never *do* do what the advertisers imply they will. You want *real* youth, *real* sex, *real* escape, and *real* companionship. So you decide to *buy* a new life.

So, at great financial cost ("I gave her *everything*! I was a *fool!*) and at great emotional cost ("The kids were bewildered, *bewildered!*"), that's just what you in fact do, you buy a chance to start over. You "give everything up" for it, but the sacrifice is not really all that great because the "everything" you're "giving up" is what you want to get shook of anyway. You *want* to begin again "more simply," as you say. But wouldn't it have been smarter to have kept it simple in the first place?

That's not the way we are, though, is it? We have the idea that it's "simpler" and "easier" to abandon whatever's not working than to stick with it and try to get it going again. Our whole economy, in fact and of course, is built on the idea of replacement rather than repair. What's happened, what explains this, is that our lives, like our machines, have gotten *so* goddamn complicated that it's not just *easier* to replace them than repair them, but it may well be we no longer know *how* to repair them at all.

All these wretched noisy machines that have entirely reshaped the pattern of our lives at work and at home— the car, the television, the telephone—they're all useful, *hatefully* useful, but ultimately we don't *like* the way they've reshaped the pattern of our lives. And all these wretched noisy "conveniences" that could do so much to help us establish a little order in our lives—all the dishwashers, washing machines, disposals, electric coffee pots, irons, dryers, knife sharpeners, grinders and blenders and mixers, vacuum cleaners, water pumps, freezers, electric alarm clocks, and so on—that are supposed to have replaced the servants of the Old Order and brought a new leisure to the home, that are supposed to do the work, *don't*. They help, maybe; but they don't *do* the work. And there are so *many* of them now that there's always at least one of them that isn't working that we have to "service." *We* service *them* almost as much as they service us.

But the point I'm making now is that no one knows how to fix things any more. Not only don't we know how to fix these things ourselves, but neither do the people who sell them to us. All they know how to do is sell us new ones. One reason, of course, is that mass-production methods require a mass-distribution system that licenses dealers as authorized maintenance and repair agents. So of course when you phone a dealer to repair something, he's going to sell you a new one instead. He knows a conflict of interest when he sees one. This has reached the point, though, where he isn't *able* to repair the things, even if he wanted to, which of course he doesn't.

Whenever one does somehow manage to get a thing repaired everyone admits it is better than new. When the motor on my new furnace went bad, still within the guarantee period (the manufacturer had miscalculated by a few weeks), honest Mr. O'Keefe who sold it to me told me it was better to have it repaired under the guarantee than replaced: the sheer fact of some human attention to these machines strengthens them; the new motors are so shoddily-skimpily made that in order to repair them one simply has to use better, stronger materials—it's impossible not to. But the non-dealer repairman is an economic anachronism; and as they go out of business, one after the other, the whole concept of fixing or repairing vanishes from American life right along with them.

One accommodates to this, of course, or tries to outwit it as best one can. One buys a TV cheap enough to begin with, so that when it goes out of order one can afford to throw it away and get a new one. I haven't in my whole life ever owned a decent watch—a watch like my father's or grandfather's that was a pleasure for them to consult, to wind regularly, to handle, to fondle even. All I've ever owned is a succession of rather nasty Timexes, purchased for six or eight dollars—they are disposable watches. Accommodating to modern life means accepting the shoddy and expendable instead of enjoying the valuable and permanent.

There are analogies here, you know. I'm not just running off about the machines, although they really do bug me and they really are a part of the problem as well as analogous to it. Makes me like the noisy things more than I have in years, now I think of it, this new rhetorical utility they've developed. Very well then, *to the analogies!*: It appears, to begin with, that nowadays we can "buy" a new life for ourselves, just as we can buy a new anything else if we're getting tired of it or it doesn't seem to be working too well. Then it seems that modern marriages are as expendable as mass-produced machines; they seem in fact to have a built-in obsolescence factor like our autos: they last about six to eight years—more if it's a cream puff, less if you get a lemon. Also, like the modern machines, which are far and away too complicated for any normal ordinary man to fix, our modern lives get so complicated that even the specialists (the lawyers, the marriage counselors, the shrinks, and so on) may tell us (as do the manufacturer, the dealer, and the repairman) that it's "simpler" to start all over with a new one.

This is modern all the way; you can't deny it, and even to deplore it is out-of-date. The best we can hope to do with our lives and marriages is try not to let them get too run down in the first place. As with the modern complex machines you can't repair once they break, the thing to do is *maintain* them, maintain the *order* of them, maintain them *in* order, maintain them in *good* order.

Those vending machines on the platforms in the New York City subway system keep coming into my mind. I hate having them there—in my mind, that is, as well as on the platforms. You don't suppose it's the first beginnings of some science-fiction "scheme of the machines" to infiltrate and destroy the minds of those who attack them? Why would they start with me? I think it's just that they seem to me—these subway vending machines do—some kind of metaphor for the relationship between our disordered commercial society and the individuals who comprise it. Conceived for pure profit in sheer mindlessness, they exist in chaos. If they were working they'd sell you a plastic bag of stale cashews or a tasteless, undersized candy-bar. If they were working they'd take trade away from the human being who runs the candy-counter news-stand at the subway-stop entrance. If they were working they'd be "a convenience" only if you had the required exact change, which you'd just plain lose if you put it in the way things are now. For these machines are not, of course and in fact, *ever* working. Like four out of five of the new outdoor telephone booths that are supposed to be a convenient innovation in the most modern city in the world, they all say:

OUT OF ORDER

which is perhaps *the* sign of our times.

PART TWO

The Revelations of a Fussy Man

"Nobody," *said reasonably,*
He ~~whimpered,~~
"Could call me
A fussy man;
I *only* want
A little bit
Of butter for
My bread!"

—A. A. MILNE
"The King's Breakfast"

How and When Properly to Make and Eat Milk Toast

I WON'T ATTEMPT TO DISGUISE THE FACT THAT MILK TOAST is simply toast—buttered, sprinkled with sugar, eaten with warmed milk in a bowl. Admittedly, milk toast is an undeceptively simple dish; but, as is true of all Life's Activities (with no exception I can think of), it is important that a thing be done *right* for full enjoyment to occur. In fact, a good deal of the pleasure of milk toast lies therein—that is, in planning the best method of preparing it and eating it, and then executing the plan with precision.

Milk toast, perhaps more than any other dish, requires a sense of occasion. There is a proper time to have it; and while that time is often Sunday-night supper, it isn't *always* then or *only* then. There are other occasions when it's just right to say to your wife, as she's preparing supper: "No big dinner for me tonight—I'll just have a little milk toast." The thing is to make sure that what the rest of the family is having is something you don't much like. There's scarcely pleasure in eating something when you know that what's on your plate isn't as good as what's on everyone else's plate at the table. In a family everyone usually has to eat the same thing, which is why the family has survived as an institution. But in a restaurant, of course, what the other people order is always better. In Europe one summer with my family, I went the whole time—every night in a different hotel dining room—without ever once having ordered something as good as what the rest of them had. It got so that when I'd sometimes choose the same thing as one of the children, the child would change his order. My family now says that that's the reason we never go anywhere any more, which isn't true. But at least when I make milk toast at home, they know I'm having something I like more than they like what they're having.

Now for the recipe.

You will need the following: a table and chair, a small cereal bowl, a matching plate to go underneath it (this is needed, no matter how informal you want to be—I'll explain it later), a soup spoon, a thin-necked milk jug, a saucepan, a stove, perhaps a toaster (more about toasting in a minute), a napkin (a paper napkin will do, but a cloth one is a pleasure in itself), a sugar bowl and sugar spoon, and (of course) sugar, milk, bread, and butter.

Bread first. Most American bread is so soft in the middle that it makes a soggy milk toast. French bread or Italian bread is of no use for milk toast, for while it may indeed be sliced and toasted, it doesn't really make *toast* —at least not in the sense we Americans think of toast. The ideal would be British bread, but that is of course not available in this country. Nevertheless, something must be done, if we are to have milk toast at all! The remedy in this case is simpler than the difficulty: simply get Pepperidge Farm white bread, or Arnold's Hearthstone, or one such of those "better" breads available at your local grocery store.

Be assured, we're not going to find everything so easy!

The slices of bread should be toasted (three slices are required, for just the right amount of milk toast). I myself do not favor a pop-up toaster: it fails to dry the bread sufficiently, because the heat is applied simultaneously on both sides. Also, it reduces the challenge and difficulty involved in *getting things right* since the toaster works automatically on a timer principle. Granted there is some pleasure in adjusting the timer *exactly* to the way one likes toast, but when this goal is once achieved (and surely it can't take more than a month or two, as one has all sorts of other occasions to be making toast) then the challenge is gone.

Best is an old-fashioned flip-flop sort of toaster that toasts the bread on one side, and often rather unevenly. This requires that you constantly take the bread out and turn it, so that it gets done evenly on the corners. Very satisfying work, as it needs constant attention and utmost concentration if you do two pieces at the same time—as you ought, for the challenge of it.

I said before that a toaster might not be necessary at all. That is because your average stove has a broiler, which will toast bread nicely—especially an electric stove, which applies a very even heat. The thing here is to watch the toast constantly, bending or squatting if necessary to peer into the broiler, or perhaps drawing up a kitchen chair to be comfortable. The broiler has the added advantage of doing three pieces of toast at once, which few toasters are able to do. Incidentally, if you *are* using the toaster, do the single slice of bread first, as there will then be only one to cool off while the other two are toasting. Not a thing many people think of, but a helpful hint.

Heat, however, isn't as important for the toast as it is for the milk—so it's not even that much of a hint. The important thing with the toast is that it be *crisp*. The only satisfactory way to keep toast crisp is in a toast rack, which is not used in this country. It is a small nickel-plated rack that holds the toast upright, the slices side-by-side and separated from one another, and the toast gets hard and dry while sitting in it instead of soft and mushy as it does when piled slice on slice. In England, even the seediest bed-and-breakfast hotels have one for each table, and it is hard to understand how our country, a land supposedly based on plenty and convenience, should go without what is really such a necessity. Toast racks, though, are absolutely impossible to buy in America, and of course it really isn't worth an inconvenient trip all the way to England just to buy one. So I'd hardly know how to advise someone who was without. Perhaps he may have a friend in England who will mail him one.

Never butter the toast ahead of time. To my knowledge, prebuttered toast is seen only in the coffeeshops of out-of-town hotels. The butter should be moderately hard, and should be carefully applied to the toast in thin chunks, never spread. Do not use sweet butter; use the routine, lightly salted kind. After buttering one piece of toast, put it on the cereal bowl, resting it on the rim so that the four corners stick out evenly over the round edge.

Now, the sugar. The sugar should be in its own bowl, along with the sugar spoon (larger than a teaspoon, smaller than a tablespoon, not a soup spoon—but a Regular Sugar Spoon, the one that should always be in the sugar bowl). Never, incidentally, allow others in the family to use this spoon for stirring, say, coffee. With such indiscriminate use, sugar subsequently cakes on the spoon, and droplets of coffee get in the sugar bowl and form nasty brown lumps. It's easy enough to pick them out of the bowl—rather fun, in fact—but then one never knows what to do with them. Of course you could put them in your own coffee, but one rather hates to, because they look as if the sugar had *already* been used. You could put them on your butter plate, but individual butter plates are not much used any more; they seem to have disappeared at about the same time as the nice butter balls made with wooden paddles. True, one could put the little coffee-sugar pebbles in the saucer of one's own cup; but with the lifting of one's own cup, the pebbles tend to roll down into the saucer's center, so that when one's cup is put back down it mashes the sugar, and if there is any moisture whatsoever on the outside of the cup (of course there shouldn't be, but things are not always the way they should be in this world—as an old philosophy professor said to me, "You can't get an *is* out of an *ought!*"), it very shortly makes for the sort of sticky mess that takes four or five minutes to straighten out, and meanwhile the coffee is cooling.

But never mind about all that at the moment. It shouldn't have been mentioned in the first place.

Now, however, carefully remove the lid from the sugar bowl, placing it to one side, and then lift out from three quarters of a teaspoon to a level teaspoonful of sugar. Do not under any circumstances take out a rounded or (God

41

forbid!) heaping teaspoonful, as some grains are bound to spill on the trip from the sugar bowl to the milk toast bowl, no matter how careful one is. Heaping teaspoonfuls are an anathema anyway! It is repugnant to imagine the sort of impatient mentality that conceived of the heaping teaspoonful in the first place.

A piece of toast may be considered, for all useful intents and purposes, square. The rounded, "upper" edge can be left out of consideration, really—although I cannot deny myself the indulgence of mentioning that I myself find it nice to have the piece of toast arranged on the bowl so that the rounded edge is away from me—just as I like to have the pointed part of a piece of pie facing toward me. It's very satisfying to arrange the toast that way, perhaps even using two hands, and then lean back and contemplate it.

One mustn't enjoy anticipation for too long, for meanwhile the milk is cooling. The problem now is to sprinkle the sugar onto the piece of toast *evenly*. Certainly no one wants all the sugar to be in the middle of his piece of milk toast, with little or none at all on the crusty corners. And yet, how difficult it is to get it right! When you go to sprinkle the corners, some of the sugar is bound to tumble over the sides and even outside the bowl. It is for this reason that there must be a plate under the bowl. (I mentioned earlier that I would give the reason!)

But plate or no plate, the sprinkling of the sugar is a difficult business. To do it, one rapidly agitates the spoon from side to side, causing the grains to fly off onto whatever is being sprinkled. What a risk, and so unlike the fastidious care involved in spreading. (In fact, sprinkling and spreading are at the opposite poles of human behavior.)

Of course, instead of sprinkling the sugar on the toast, one *could* place it there carefully, tilting the spoon and edging it off. I find this has the practical disadvantage of getting too much sugar on the toast, and the emotional disadvantage of making the tilter look a bit obsessed in the eyes of his family. It's not really proper for children to have to watch while their father, a wild gleam in his eye, fusses to get the sugar grains to do right.

Few sights in this world can be so pleasing as a piece of toast sitting on the bowl, evenly sprinkled with sugar, all waiting and ready to receive warm milk. The milk should be routine homogenized milk, heated carefully in a saucepan on the stove until it is as hot as it can be without boiling. It is hard to know just how much milk to prepare for three slices of toast. Depending on my mood, I heat as little as seven eighths of a cupful or as much as a cupful and one eighth. Somewhere in there is just right.

At any rate, the heated milk should be carefully poured from the saucepan into a thin-necked jug or pitcher which has been preheated with hot water to take the chill off it. This jug or pitcher is thin-necked so as to expose only a small area of the milk to the cooling air. Also—and this is perhaps the single nasty thing about milk toast—there is a scum that sometimes forms on hot milk. It's perhaps just as well to speak of it as little as possible. Suffice to say that the thinner-necked the jug is, the less surface there will be for this unpleasant layer to form on.

Pouring the milk onto the toast is as perilous as sprinkling on the sugar. It is not as difficult, but the consequences of careless action are much more dire. Sprinkle the sugar carelessly and you have a few grains of displaced sugar. Pour the milk too abruptly, and it bounces off the toast and over the side of the bowl and you've got a puddle of milk in the plate or (God forbid) on the table. Should this ever happen, I suppose that what one would do is take the whole mess to the kitchen sink and start all over again—for by the time you'd wiped everything up, the original piece of toast would be too soggy to eat. Fortunately, I've never experienced this, although I suppose I will someday. I think about it every time I lift the milk jug to pour.

A gentle tipping of the pitcher, and we will be ready to eat our milk toast. After about a third of the pitcher's contents have been poured on, the toast will soften in the middle and sink slowly into the bowl.

Milk toast should be eaten with great relish, otherwise there isn't much point in it. With the edge of the soup spoon cut pieces out of the middle, trying to get an equal amount of butter and sugar on each spoonful of milk and toast you eat. The four crusts should curl up somewhat out of the milk, so they will remain crisp longest and should be eaten last. When that piece of toast is finished, the milk in the bowl should be finished too, so that all will be fresh and in readiness for the next piece of toast. With a little experience this can be easily managed, and by the time the third piece is eaten, the pitcher should be dry.

Easy, isn't it? As I made clear at the very outset, making and eating milk toast is one of the simplest things in the world to do. Compare it with some other of Life's Activities—making oyster stew, for instance, or preparing for a family picnic, or arranging a liaison. Everything is monstrously complicated these days, *except for milk toast*. Indeed, it is milk toast's very simplicity that makes it so attractive; it is one of the few things that can be done really right.

From time to time, though, my enjoyment in milk toast is a bit soured by the realization that it is such a solitary pleasure. Sometimes in my imagination I am part of a huge farm-family all eating milk toast at once. I envision a long toast rack that runs the whole length of the table, and three sugar bowls (to minimize passing), and a giant milk jug within the reach of each person. How jolly it would be! An old-fashioned family, all carefully eating milk toast together, and no one spilling!

❀ *How to Know Whether to Get Up and Fix the Way the Television Picture Is Revolving or Wait and See if It Fixes Itself*

THIS IS A SERIOUS PROBLEM, OF COURSE, FOR THE ESSENCE of television watching is being able to sit there inertly, and having to get up spoils the point of the whole thing. Also, of course, if one fixes it, it may start revolving worse, faster, the other way. What makes matters so perplexing, again of course, is that if you wait, the television keeps on doing it; while if you get up, it stops doing it just as you walk toward it. The point of particular anguish is that there's no way of knowing if it would have stopped if you hadn't gotten up.

I firmly believe that it wouldn't have stopped. It's not the perversity of "things," but just that it really does help the TV when you walk toward it. No personification of an inanimate object is intended here—if I believed for one minute that our television acts the way it does because of having any sort of personality, I'd chuck it out of the house tomorrow. I believe that your body being near the thing acts as some kind of extra antenna, in a *technical* way; and that's what makes it stop revolving when you get up. Reasoning about it would then seem to lead to the conclusion that you must get up and not wait to see if it fixes itself. But before you get up, for heaven's sake notice which way it is revolving, so that when it stops revolving as you approach it, you can remember which way the adjustment has to be made. Do it carefully, just a little, so that it doesn't start going the other way. Then start backing away from it gently, never taking your eyes off it, until you are standing with the back of your legs pressed against the seat of your chair. Then bend your knees quickly, pretending to sit down, then snap straight up again. If it remains steady, then you can try actually sitting, lowering yourself very gradually and gently. But then of course it sees what you have done, and it may start doing it again, either the same way or the other way.

With a slight up-and-down motion of neck and chin, it is perfectly possible to follow what's going on. And when it gets stuck in the middle, all you have to do is remember that the bottom half of the picture is really the top of the frame and just switch it up there in your mind's eye. Of course, you can try stamping your foot at it to try to get it going again by the jolt effect, which is what the kids do; but I think it takes that as a loss of temper and only encourages it—and besides, if you do get it going again, is it that much better?

Finally, you can try pretending to get up, but I don't think that works because it has a very big eye and sees right into your mind. The best thing to do, ultimately, is just shut your eyes and listen, peeking every once in a while to see if it has fixed itself.

❈ *How to Organize a Family Picnic (and Keep It That Way)*

HAPPY FAMILY PICNICS ARE ALL ALIKE; EVERY UNHAPPY family picnic is unhappy in its own way.

Everything is confusing in the household about to go on an unhappy family picnic. Nothing is ready. Chances are someone must be sent on a last-minute trip to the store, or to borrow some piece of equipment; and he takes forever getting back and the expedition gets off to a late start, the fine weather now beginning to cloud over. Undoubtedly the family goes to an ill-chosen destination, too crowded or perhaps much farther away than they'd thought it was. Surely they have too much to carry in one trip from the car. There are ants, flies, mosquitoes, gnats, no-see-ums, or the possibility of snakes. The water is too muddy for swimming, or the surf too high. There aren't enough of the chicken sandwiches; no one likes the peanut butter and jelly there *is* enough of. There are arguments over whose fault it was they forgot vital things. They run out of soft drinks and the children have to sip beer. Maybe the touch football game turns serious and ends in injury or bad feeling. Children nag and drop their food in the sand, it seems deliberately. Teen-agers are bored or disgusted, it's hard to tell which. The grandparents want to start home almost as soon as they've arrived; they think there's a storm coming, and they may be right. The baby, who would never have been brought if they could have found a sitter, has been crying constantly. The other children are cold, wet, sunburned, irritable, about to start screaming and fighting; there's no extra sweater for them, much less a change of clothes. Everyone now wants to go home, but they have to wait for Father, who went off two hours ago with a French girl in a bikini, someone's houseguest, way down the beach out of sight. Who can blame him? But when they get back he makes no explanation, just gives a foolish grin, and everyone's furious. The family must surely get lost on the way back home; it seems to all of them as if the trip is lasting forever. When they come in at last—sandy in the crotch, hot under the collar, sunburned and headachy and sick to death of one another's attitude—they drop whatever they carry in from the car just anywhere. The parents have completely missed a cocktail party they'd promised to go to, are already late for dinner at the home of new friends. But the children, somehow too tired to be sleepy, now say they are hungry again. Nothing whatsoever can be done in the kitchen, though, until the mess from the picnic has been cleaned up and at least some of all the stuff that was just dumped there has been put away. No one has anything remotely like the strength or the good temper to do all that needs to be done to reestablish order in the house. Of course, not all these things may happen on even the most unhappy family picnic, but there's a variety of other worse things that may. Every unhappy family picnic is unhappy in its own way.

On the other hand, happy family picnics are all alike. There's a delicious luncheon, plenty of fried chicken prepared the day before, and lots of other good things, all carefully and lovingly packed in neat, easy-to-carry containers, nothing forgotten, transported by car or boat to a charming picnic site, in beautiful sunny weather, a Bloody Mary for those that want it, the food relished after a refreshing swim; then a friendly game of touch football, full of laughs; kindly teen-agers helping happy children make sand castles, as doting grandparents fondly watch; an easy agreement about when to leave; a quick and uneventful trip home; everything put back neatly where it belongs; and life resumes its normal schedule. That's the kind of happy family picnic that's worth going on.

And there's only one real difference between a happy family picnic and an unhappy family picnic. No, it has nothing to do with the family. Nor is it a matter of luck. It's organization. If you want to have a happy family picnic, you have to organize one, and then keep it that way.

Now that isn't to say that an amount of confusion and excitement isn't basic to any family picnic, happy or unhappy. An amount of confusion is in some way the *point* of a picnic—when a family deliberately disrupts its ordinary meal-taking routine in favor of a festive outing, the attendant "confusion" is almost "normal"; it is anyway deliberately created. But this confusion shouldn't be allowed to turn to chaos. Deliberately created human chaos is the nature of war, not the family picnic. When the touch football starts to get rough, it's necessary to get the good players all on one side, where they'll enjoy playing skillfully together; and against them—three or four against ten or a dozen, say—pit the whole rest of the family, inept, good-natured, unmotivated in this area, thoroughly willing to lose. Touch football games, life itself, families themselves, picnics *them*selves, and family picnics in particular and peculiar—all have great tendencies toward chaos. It's my great belief, although I seldom dare say it because I know it sounds excessive or obsessive, maybe both, that getting things in general somehow just a bit more organized might very well be one of the great secrets of virtue and happiness in life—or it could be, I mean, if we were ever able to do it.

REFINING THE PROBLEM

You know, don't you, that organizing a family picnic is not just taking your wife and kids on a picnic? I'd assume you knew how to do that yourself. There's got to be more than just the so-called "nuclear" family involved. But the "extended" family being what it is today—shrunken, scattered, differentiated—it may be necessary to concoct your family picnic out of two or more families. Getting a whole bunch of friends or neighbors, with their children and houseguests, all together to go on a picnic with you, or even meeting them at the picnic site independently, has got to be considered as organizing a family picnic—or at least "a reasonable facsimile thereof," as they used to say of boxtops on the radio—because when several households are involved the planning and scheduling can really get just as complicated, and the event itself just as chaotic, as in a true, large, old-fashioned, multibranched single-family family picnic.

But just because members of different families may sometimes be included, don't get the idea a family picnic bears any resemblance to those jolly beach parties and barbecues you see on television advertisements, where a lot of young people are all laughing and splashing and having a great time. One of the reasons they're all laughing and splashing and having a great time, I'm convinced, is that they're all using the same brand of thing—Pepsi or Budweiser or whatever—and didn't have to lug a lot of different stuff. It's the sameness of them in general that makes them different. They're all good-looking and popular; but that they're all the same age is the important thing. God maybe made family resemblances, but he never yet made a family where everyone was the same age. Families nowadays may or may not be cohesive, but they are very seldom coherent, in the sense that each member of the picnic has the same expectations for it, the way all the teen-agers at the TV soft-drinks orgy do. A family picnic is like a wedding or a funeral, only without such a sense of purpose—and we all know how out of hand wakes and receptions can get, when all those people who have known each other too long and too well get together. It's hard for members of a family to get along, fond as they are of one another. In order to have this intermittent, nonoccasional, midsummer, midday, semiceremonial sort of tribal gathering, a movable feast in ways no religious calendar could intend, it is necessary for everyone to give way to everyone else a little. Everyone has to bend a little—and anyone who's bending, especially in a family, is always under tension to snap back.

Into this situation—admittedly somewhat laughable, but still genuinely ticklish—now must step the leader of the picnic. Will it be you?

POWER AND THE PICNIC

Guests usually have a better time at a family picnic than anyone else—they have few expectations about how it should all be, no ideas of their own about it to get thwarted, no burdensome sense of responsibility for the picnic's success or failure. What appears to be the power vacuum of the chaotic family picnic is in fact usually the opposite: not lack of leadership, but too much; not too few leaders, but the inability of a single one to assume control. Many members of the family have their own ideas about how the picnic should be run—sometimes it seems all of them do. And because it's a family that's involved, not an army or a business or anything like that, there's no way to establish discipline, you can't fire them or demote them. They're all family members and feel they have their rights. They're all in a position to dispute your decisions every step of the way—*every step of the way,* from whether or not to take a particular beach blanket in the first place, to whereabouts on the beach is the best place to put it down. Since there's no such thing as unquestioned leadership on a family picnic, if you do become the organizer you'll have the pleasure (or the consolation) of knowing that your leadership qualities are being supremely tested, forged in the white-hot furnace of family contention, tempered by the easygoing way you have to act. It is a role far more liable to recrimination than to appreciation, a dire responsibility year in and year out, involving not only the well-known loneliness of command but also people constantly bugging you with questions. You will also have to go on most all the picnics yourself. "We couldn't *do* it without you," they may say after a while. This sense of your own indispensability will be one of your few rewards.

So if you can, then you must. If you have the necessary skills and experience, in logics and logistics, as dietician, auto packer, boatsman, games organizer, diplomat, weather forecaster, and so on, and if you don't mind spending the morning on the phone trying to straighten out misconceptions about the picnic and being enthusiastic about it—then you must do it yourself. You owe it to your family to take on this task, as men who run for the Presidency are recognizing their obligation to the nation. Take *absolute* control, if you can. Remember this—although it may sound totalitarian to you—that the more you can keep the others in the role of guests, the more likely they are to enjoy the picnic.

THE PREPARE COMMITTEE

I sometimes dream of a bureaucratic solution to the picnic power problem—a special committee for Picnic Recruiting, Exhorting, Provisioning, Authorizing, Regulating, and Expediting—The PREPARE Committee, I call it in my imagination. It is a sort of Planning and Operations Board comprised of the more sensible and effective members of the family without regard to their actual autocratic age and rank, or even their niceness. This informal committee, because of its absolute efficiency, would gradually gain absolute control of all aspects of family picnic planning, cutting across all the normal lines of authority and control. One member of The Committee would be in charge of coordinating Provisions; another for coordinating Transportation; another could be on Communications and Scheduling; and so on. Because they had all the information, everyone would have to come to them for decisions. All such questions as "What can *we* bring?" and "Will you have room for the three of us in the sailboat?" and "When and where shall we meet you?" would thus be referred to the appropriate PREPARE Committee member for an immediate and accurate answer, instead of being answered by just whoever happens to pick up the phone, who always gives a lot of wrong information and never tells anybody. The Committee would have sole charge of Authorizing expeditions, and in return for this power, freely (or perhaps even reluctantly) granted to them by the family as a whole, they would be expected and required to stamp out wildcat, brushfire picnics suggested by individual family members on a spur-of-the-moment basis.

All of this is daydreaming, of course. No one would want to be on The PREPARE Committee if all it meant were a lot of draggy work; and if it turned out for some reason to have any power or to be fun, every member of the family would want some role in it, which would put you back where you started, and if they didn't get a role, someone would start a rival family picnic organizing group. One has to be more realistic: the best ideas are the ones you have to abandon first, if you're working with people.

SIX TRUSTY SERVING MEN

Fortunately, instead of The PREPARE Committee, you have your Six Trusty Serving Men to help you organize your happy family picnic. You remember them, I'm sure, from your happy childhood:

> I have six trusty serving men;
> They taught me all I knew.
> Their names are *what* and *why* and *when*
> And *where* and *how* and *who*.

They'll help you decide who will come on your family picnic, where to go, how to get there, what to take, when to go and come back, and maybe even shed some light on why you're going.

WHY

The point of a family picnic is that you're doing this thing *together*. More and more nowadays the generations are separated; "gapped" is the term used, I believe. The urbanization, bureaucratization, and industrialization of America are destroying the family as a value-providing institution. Everyone goes his separate way: it is an *atomized* society we live in. The point of a family picnic is to bring the family together to have a picnic together.

WHO

The rationale of the family picnic thus determines the personnel of the family picnic: in theory, everyone has to come, or else be made to feel slightly guilty about not going. All the generations must be there, too. A picnic is really kind of pointless without the littlest kind of children to watch playing in the sand and worry about. A picnic needs adolescents to raise the achievement level in touch football and so one can worry about them swimming out too far. It needs middle-aged people to over-exert so people can worry about that. And it needs older people to do most of the worrying, although they can be worried about too, by the others. Worrying about others is an important aspect of the happy family picnic.

WHERE

A family picnic, you know, is not just a backyard barbecue—you have to *go* somewhere, and not just to someone else's backyard; that's just an outdoor party. Every family has at least two places they picnic more or less regularly, one near and one far—and the farther one is always better. If there are more than two places, then the best one is always farthest away of them all. This appears to be one of Life's Cruel Truths, but it really can be more easily understood: for no family in its right mind would travel *farther* to picnic in a *worse* place, and especially not farth*est* to picnic in *the* worst place. A happy family picnic will seldom if ever go anyplace new—the hazards are too great, the expectations too varied. Tried and true places are the best, even if people are a bit sick of them. Tradition and continuity are also important aspects of the family picnic.

HOW

As to "how to go," this is arguable mainly on the basis of who gets to go in which car or boat with whom. For many young children this may represent their first experience with DCG—the Dyscohesion of Companionable Groups. A child will often complain about the car or boat he's assigned to, saying he'd rather be in one of the other ones with his cousins rather than his siblings, or with his siblings rather than his cousins, or whatever. What's required here is a simple matter of education: the child has just not lived long enough to understand how things are. Explain to him that this *is* one of Life's Cruel Truths—that *no one* ever wants to ride with the people he has to ride with; the fun people are *always* in the other boat. That's in the nature of things, tell him, an LCT. When you get older and get to go to dinner parties, child, the people you want to talk with are always seated at the other end of the table, where all the laughing is. One of the main reasons we *have* family picnics, child, is so that you can learn about life. Education of the young in the ways of adults is a prime aspect of family picnics.

THE "TF," OR TRANSFERRAL FACTOR

"How to go" also provides the Transferral Factor, which is a major determinant, in turn, of "what to take." Children and mothers and others will sometimes want to bring along something "extra."—a beach ball, say, or a bag full of knitting—casually explaining, "Oh, let's take such-and-such, just in case we want it." Don't let a child persuade you with the line, "I promise I'll carry it myself"; make it clear to him that if he's carrying *that,* then he won't be able to carry something that's necessary. Point out that the act of taking this one other thing seems easy now, but it must be multiplied by the Transferral Factor. The TF varies from picnic to picnic, depending on how you go. It can perhaps be as low as four: taking whatever it is from the house to the car, *one;* from the car to the picnic, *two;* from the picnic back to the car, *three;* from the car back into the house, *four.* But a TF of four is the absolute minimum. In some cases the TF can be quite frightening. If it's a question of transferring all the stuff from the house to the car to a dock to a dinghy, and from the dinghy into a big boat, then from the big boat back into the dinghy and from the dinghy to the landing place, then carrying it all to the picnic site—plus doing it all back the other way—you get a TF of fourteen.

And with a TF that high, you must be very stern about the "what."

WHAT

While everybody knows that a lot has to be taken on a family picnic, few realize just *what* a lot. Just to begin with, there are Frisbees, beach balls, footballs, whiffle balls (and whiffle bats); snorkels, flippers, and masks; huge hats, for the shade; sweaters for all, in case it gets chilly; slickers, in case of rain or spray; a change of clothing for the children on the way home; a different bottle or tube of a different brand or kind of suntan lotion for each and every female family picnicker; mustard; sneakers or flip-flops for the hot sand; shovels and pails for the littlest; bathing suits and bathing caps, of course; rubber rafts and surfboards and truck-tire inner tubes; beach mats, beach towels, beach chairs, beach umbrellas, beach blankets, beach bags, and L. L. Bean carry-alls; something to read; sunglasses; life jackets for the safety of the little ones and life jackets for all for the sake of the Coast Guard; knives and forks and spoons and paper cups and paper plates; charcoal, hibachi, and charcoal-lighter fluid, or else wood, kindling, and newspaper, for the beaches are picked clean of driftwood by midsummer; and matches; also lots of cigarettes, enough for the people who forget to bring an extra pack; a bottle opener; combs; and lots and lots of other stuff I've forgotten. For instance, I think I've forgotten the food. And I've also forgotten—perhaps deliberately but it would be disaster if we didn't bring it—the most cumbersome thing of all, the most recent inevitability of the family picnic: a giant styrofoam chest, light in itself, but heavy beyond credence with ice and slopping water and beer and soda pop, with a shifty center of gravity and a double handle excruciating after six steps on the sand. Even the gone-but-not-forgotten (and certainly-not-lamented) Scotch Cooler seems lighter than this in memory.

I've often wanted to mimeograph up a Family Picnic Comprehensive Master Checklist to make sure nothing would be forgotten, but I know something would be forgotten anyway. Someone would check the thing off, *intending* to put it in the basket, and then forget; or she might actually put it in all right and then take it out later to make things fit better and *then* forget to put it back in. In some way or other, something would be forgotten. Checklists and systems and organizings are fine, just so long as you don't apply them to human beings. Unfortunately, though, that's all they're for, is for human beings; they have no other use whatsoever, so far as I can see—except, of course, for the fun of making them up.

WHEN

Once on a big multifamily family picnic on Napatree Point, off Watch Hill, Rhode Island, a good, happy, boating-swimming picnic on a gorgeous Saturday afternoon, I was talking with an eight-year-old I really like, name of Alexander Lichtenstein, and he was running on about how much fun this was and how we ought to have another picnic real soon. Finally he asks, "When *can* we come again?"

"How about tomorrow?" I said.

"No," he says. "That's *too* soon."

Even children realize that you can't have a picnic every day. It's not just that they're too exhausting, too much exercise all at once, too much scrambled brains and sunburn from the hot sun, too much work and time and disruption, but also that they're somehow too much fun, the happy ones, at least; they must remain as an "occasion" that is somehow special.

Planning a family picnic a week or so in advance is good for the anticipation of the event, so that people won't make other plans, for the time to prepare, and so on; but it is bad because one can never be sure what the weather will be. Ideally you should have such a good family picnic organizational cadre set up that no advance planning would be necessary. "It looks like a beautiful day . . . ," you ought to be able to say in a certain alerting tone at breakfast. There's a sudden, dramatic hush at the table; everyone looks at you expectantly, hopefully. "So, let's go on a picnic," you say, releasing the tension with a smile. Instantly they go into action: one person leaps to phone the prearranged list of family picnic members; two others are off in the car to the grocery store with the preprepared shopping list; others as preassigned, put on the hard-boiled eggs, do the breakfast dishes, get out the ice, pack the always-ready fried chicken from the freezer, get out the baskets and blankets and so on; the whole family swinging into motion like a well-oiled machine. You should be ready to leave within an hour if you want, two at the most; but the decision still has to be made as to exactly when.

ESTABLISHING THE ETD

Before you can decide what time to go on a picnic, you need to know what time you want to get back home. The secret of good planning is looking ahead and then calculating backward. Say you want to be home at 4:45 P.M. You know it takes fifteen minutes to put everything away when you get home, half an hour to get back from the picnic place, and another fifteen minutes to pick up all the stuff at the picnic place and pack it neatly in the car for the return journey—a total of one hour. So you want to leave the picnic place for home at 3:45 P.M. Suppose you want two hours to have your picnic or enjoy it or whatever you plan to do with it. Thus you should arrive at the picnic place at 1:45. That's your ETA. To find your Estimated Time of Departure, subtract forty-five more minutes (how long it takes you to get from home to the picnic place and get unpacked). Thus ETD is 1 P.M., or 1300 hours. And if anyone objects that thirteen hundred is just when you ought to have lunch, tell him (or her) that it's all been worked out systematically and stop eggbeating.

THE COUNTDOWN

For an ETD of 1300, you'll want to begin your countdown at noon. Call out loudly to the whole household: "Sixty minutes to ETD." For the first half hour call out the time remaining in five-minute intervals: "Fifty-five minutes to ETD," "Fifty minutes," and so on. For the first twenty-five minutes of the remaining half hour, call it out each minute: "Thirty minutes to ETD," "Twenty-nine minutes to ETD," and so on, down to "Five minutes to ETD."

For most of the second half hour, probably, and certainly for what follows, it is best to get a child to hold the watch and do the calling, as loudly and enthusiastically as possible. These final moments should be scary for everyone—leader and led alike. The leader has planned well: he knows the women are not as likely to turn on the child as on himself. But there's always the possibility of revolt at this key moment, or—even worse—the women may just ignore the countdown. So if he sees they're pretty far behind, the leader may adjust the countdown to the situation, telling the child to put it on hold for a few minutes. "ETD minus three minutes and *holding!*" shouts the child every once in a while. Then, for the last few minutes, down to one-minute-to-go, the child should call out every five seconds: "Two minutes and fifty-five seconds remaining to ETD!" "Two minutes and *fifty* seconds!" and so on, down to *"One minute to ETD!"* This should be the really scary moment. From this point on, the child simply calls out the seconds remaining.

At the beginning of this final phase of the countdown, or perhaps a bit earlier if it is getting too tense in the house, one takes one's position behind the steering wheel of the car, getting ready to start sounding the horn at the moment for blastoff. Meanwhile, the child follows the women around the kitchen or wherever they are, packing and preparing things as fast as they can. It really speeds them up to have a child shouting: "Twenty-eight seconds," "Twenty-seven seconds," and so on.

FINAL MOMENTS

At the car, you are checking over what is being brought out of the house to go on the picnic: trying to tell what's been forgotten; trying to see if too much is being brought, in violation of the proscriptions of The Transferral Factor.

It is often in these final moments that your family-picnic leadership qualities are most crucially tried. You will learn now whether the training and discipline you've established will hold up under this climactic pressure, whether your methods of preparation and organization are going to pay off.

That's because it's a good idea at this point, if you're truly devoted to organizational efficiency and if you've got the outstanding leadership qualities required for this exercise, to take the family through an operational dry run. After everything has been packed, and the whole family is sitting there in the car all ready and waiting to go on the picnic, get them all to get out of the car again, *as if* they had arrived at the picnic place, each of them taking that which it is assigned to him to carry, so as to demonstrate to you that they can indeed handle in one load, one "trip," everything that needs to be transferred. If there is anything left over that they are not able to manage, patiently repeat the ten or fourteen stages of The Transferral Factor to them, and engage them in a calm discussion as to what part of the excess they as a group feel is least necessary to the happiness of the picnic. This is the time to use the democratic approach. The overload should then be returned to the house before departing and put carefully back where it belongs, preferably by the individual family member who was responsible for bringing it out in the first place.

This additional procedure may perhaps delay a specific departure or two until it is established as routine. It may at first be necessary to follow the faulted family member into the house and spend valuable moments persuading her that she really does want to go on the picnic, that it will be fine when we get there, that it wouldn't be any fun without her, and so on. This shouldn't be necessary, but people are funny. They want an organized picnic, but sometimes they feel they're being pushed around, or so they say. Under the guise of tradition, organization must be imposed *as the standard thing*. We know that each unhappy family picnic is unhappy in its own way, while happy family picnics are all alike. Thus, clearly: only when family picnics are so organized that they are always all alike can we be sure they're happy.

✦ *How to Be Kindly*

A FUSSY MAN IS AT A DISADVANTAGE IN HIS FAMILY NOT BE-
cause of his vices, but because of his virtues. Kindliness
is generally reckoned to be the foremost familial virtue,
and it seems to be in some sort of psychological-philo-
sophical conflict with fussiness. Occasionally in literature
you'll find some figure who combines the two—I think of
Aunt Betsy Trotwell in *David Copperfield* and what's her
name, Aunt Sally or Aunt Polly, in *Huck Finn*—but I
suppose it scarcely needs pointing out that each of these
is an *aunt,* not the man of the house, and their kindliness
is concealed anyway under what used to be known as "a
gruff exterior," something no one goes for these days.

Sloppiness and kindliness, however, seem to go hand-
in-hand, to have one of those awful "natural" affinities,
like sloth and melancholy. Your tidiness, they'll tell you,
is just a manifestation of your hostility toward others. But
if we take an orderly approach to this matter, I think we
can out-fox them.

We will assume, to begin with, that there are two kinds
of kindliness: innate and acquired. And thus there are
two ways to be kindly: naturally kindly and—uh—the op-

posite. Now it is clear that the second kind of kindliness is far superior to the first kind. There is very little credit in being innately kindly: if that's just the way you are, it wouldn't be *right* for you to get any credit for it. But a person who *forces* himself to be kindly deserves all the credit in the world. A new, learned, acquired virtue is always far shinier and better than a dull old natural one. Our Lord repeatedly says how much dearer to him is the reformed man than the one who's just naturally good. Acquired kindliness, then, is really the only kind worth having.

The first step toward becoming kindly is to *appear* kindly. You should smile sweetly a lot, more or less all the time, but especially when the children spill or anything like that. Practice your sweet smile when you're alone, in the bathroom mirror, say; and if you're sure you're alone, practice saying soothing and reassuring things like "There, there," or "Oh, don't worry about *that*," or "That's *per*fectly all right," or "How could you help it? It certainly wasn't *your* fault!" Actually, I suppose it might not be a bad idea to leave the bathroom door slightly ajar, so the family can overhear you practicing saying kind things like these—that way they'll realize how hard you're trying to be able to put up with the things they do.

What's important is to learn to say kind things so they sound really natural. If, when your wife serves your dinner, you are going to try to say something enthusiastic like, "What have I done to deserve this!?" then you've got to get the tone and emphasis exactly right or she'll misunderstand you. Apparently that's where a lot of being kindly is, in the inflection rather than the words. They tell me, for instance, that saying "How could *you* help it?" actually has something of an *un*kindly tone. At any rate, you have to be constantly on guard: people, children especially, are always on the alert for any note of sarcasm in your voice. You know how suspicious children always are.

Everyone knows that the way you act sooner or later becomes the way you are. If you *act* kindly long enough, surely you'll really *become* kindly. My wife tells me it's harder than that, but I'm convinced that it can be done. Besides, even if you can't actually manage to become kindly, people may sort of let down their guard and begin thinking of you that way. Then when you *do* get angry, they feel they've done something so terrible that they've made even kindly you lose your temper; then they feel awful about it, and you've got them where you want them.

✿ *How to Set an Alarm Clock*

IF YOU THINK IT'S SUCH A SIMPLE THING TO SET AN ALARM clock, then how come your alarm clock doesn't always go off?

A psychoanalyst would tell you it's because you don't want to get up—but I have a better explanation.

Imagine a plaza in the shape of a five-pointed star. Five men are to meet there early one morning, to go fishing or something, and they all arrive late, but simultaneously. Hurrying together in the middle, they all say apologetically in one breath (they are all out of breath): "My *alarm* didn't go off!"

"I forgot to set the clock to the right time," says man number one.

"I forgot to set when it should go off," says number two.

"I forgot to wind the clock itself," says number three.

"I forgot to wind the alarm part," says number four.

"I forgot to pull out the little knob," says number five.

They all look at one another in amazement: there are *five* things to remember when setting an alarm clock!

It's a wonder anyone's alarm clock ever goes off at all! Things are really always much more complicated than we think, even the simplest things. It isn't that we make them complicated; they *are* complicated.

Just remember the magic number "five" whenever you have to set an alarm clock. Most people, once they know there are five things to do, can figure out what the five things are—and it doesn't much matter what order they're done in. Just remember there are five things to do, and do them. Then check them, if you want. Say to yourself, "Now there were five things to do, have I done them?" Check them each over in your mind to make sure you've done them. Then look to see that each of the five has been done. Watch out that in handling the clock so much you don't inadvertently push in the little knob—the super-careful are always vulnerable to Life's Little Ironies. Check the knob, and then you'd better check the other four things again. It's nice to be certain, of course, and it hardly seems possible to check an alarm clock too many times; but don't stay up too late doing this if you have to be up early. Go to sleep secure in the knowledge that with system and care the complications of life *can* be mastered, and that your alarm will probably go off in the morning.

However . . . However, it is *modern* life we have to contend with. You don't get progress without problems, you know. The whole thrust of technology is to make conveniences more convenient, and these new conveniences can't always be solved in the old ways. You get the old alarm clock problem solved, and then they invent new, *more* convenient alarm clocks—

First, the electric alarm clock;
Second, the kind of alarm clock where when you wind the clock, you are winding the alarm at the same time.

It would seem the easiest solution to these new conveniences simply to avoid them, but it's getting harder and harder to buy an old-fashioned alarm clock. I saw an ad in the *New Yorker—*

> *The Clock That Turns Back*
> *The Clock to 1910*
>
> Pure Americana. The classic 1910 Big Ben alarm clock, handcrafted in a working, nickel-plated edition. Best gift idea of the last half century for collectors, connoisseurs and confirmed nostalgia buffs. A limited edition, at leading stores. $40.

Forty dollars?!—they used to cost a buck. Only the very rich can afford to deny progress. The rest of us have to accommodate to innovation, which means trying to outwit it.

And this isn't simply a matter of adjusting our old systems. It's not really a system anyway when you have to remember that while on an old-fashioned alarm clock there are indeed five things to do, there are on an electric clock only three—

1. Set the time;
2. Set when it's to go off;
3. Pull out the little knob—

and on the double-wind kind there are four things to do—

1, 2, 3, as above;
4. Wind the combined time and alarm.

A magic number is no longer a magic number when sometimes it's five, sometimes four, and sometimes three. The magic's gone right out of it.

71

What's needed to outwit innovation is what created it in the first place: imagination. You've got to *imagine* that you're doing all five of the magic things.

With the electric alarm clock, here's how you do it. You first set the time, *one.* If the time is already correct, as it almost always is with an electric clock, you can move the hands all the way through the twelve-hour cycle so that you feel as if you set it; or, if this seems self-indulgent to you, you can wiggle the minute hand back and forth five minutes or so each way, and then leave it set correctly. Next you set the alarm, *two.* Then you first imagine yourself winding the clock, *three.* Then you imagine yourself winding the alarm, *four.* If it helps, you can say to yourself, as you're sitting on the side of the bed, holding the clock in your hands, looking at the face of it, listening to it hum, "Now I'm winding the time part, *three;* now I'm winding the alarm part, *four.*" Then you pull out the little knob, *five.* Then you check it over, of course: "Did I remember to imagine I was winding the time? Did I remember to imagine I was winding the alarm?" and so on. Try to think of it tick-tocking coldly and mechanically as you do this; try to ignore the lifelike purring and unnaturally *warm* feeling an electric clock always has.

With the double-wind kind of alarm clock, where there is only one of those floppy little keys in the back, one which winds both the time and the alarm, the problem is a little more difficult. I bought one of these by mistake—thinking I was lucky to find a non-electric—and how wrong I was! It nearly beat me, as you'll soon see. You could do the same kind of imaginary winding that you do with the electric, but that's not terribly sensible, is it? The plain fact is, the clock actually does need winding—and imagining you're winding it as you actually *are* winding it must be ruled out as a solution. Similarly, you can't say to yourself as you're doing the necessary winding, "Now I'm winding the alarm part, *three*," and then expect yourself to turn around and just sit there holding the clock, *not* winding it, and say to yourself, "Now I'm *imagining* I'm winding the time part, *four*." Both these solutions abuse the imagination rather than use it.

Far better, clearly far more logical and more sensible, is to wind the little floppy key *halfway* tight, for *three*, and then wind it the *rest* of the way, for *four*. But this system can be used only after you've had some experience handling your clock, for there is this very great hazard in it: that you may through some bad chance wind it up tight on *three* and then not have enough wind left in it to wind for *four*.

You follow what I'm saying, don't you? You see what this danger is? All the drama of what follows depends on your understanding how it could come about and what it would mean to wind the wretched thing tight on *three* (the alarm part) and have nothing left to wind for *four* (the time part).

I admit I got quite upset when that happened to me. My wife said I went into a rage, but then she's always thinking I'm going into a rage. Actually, as I tried to tell her, it was more sorrow, or despair, that I felt, not anger at all. When I recovered, I sat on the edge of the bed thinking of all the great inventors of the world who have brought us all these nasty conveniences, and of how they had beaten me. Thomas Edison, Alexander Graham Bell, Whosit Marconi, Robert Bruce, and all the rest—men of

73

fantastic ingenuity, energy, and imagination. How could I have thought to match my solutions to their conveniences—me with my puny mind? I had stupidly wound the bloody wretched thing tight on *three,* now had no wind left for *four.* What could I do? What would they have done, faced with failure? They would have started all over again!

That's when the solution came to me: the alarm part of the clock and the time part of the clock, I deduced, must both be on the same spring if you use just one key to wind both! Immediately I set about verifying my intuition experimentally. I set the alarm for just a moment or two ahead of what time it was now, and then waited. A scary moment or two it was, too, sitting there with the thing right in my hands, waiting for it to go off. Fear of the unexpected, the thrill of the imminence of the hitherto unknown—I was experiencing all the excitement of the innovators, the explorers, and the inventors, but I was still right where I wanted to be, sitting on my own bed, working against them.

It seemed a lifetime until it finally happened, and when it did, the alarm sounded enormously loud and urgent. My wife, who had started to go back to sleep, jumped a mile, then groaned in amazement when she saw what I was doing. Nevertheless, I let the alarm run down, which took a long time because it had to unwind the time part too, of course. Then I started all over again. This time when I wound it back up I counted the number of turns of the floppy winding key—nine, it was—then made the necessary calculations, to divide nine by two, in my head. Then I set the clock to go off in a minute or two again, and waited again. It was not nearly so scary for me this time, but apparently even more disturbing to my wife. Then I let the alarm run all the way down again. Then I reset the time and the alarm, and—relishing the moment—I carefully wound the floppy key four and a half times for the alarm part. *"Three,"* I whispered, then saw she was awake watching me, and I might as well have spoke out loud. Finally, I wound the floppy key four and a half more times for the time part, pleased that I felt it wind up tight. *"Four!"* I cried in triumph.

Then I went to sleep, certain that everything was as it ought to be, with the clock at least. And my satisfaction with this achievement was so great that it scarcely bothered me when I discovered, late the next morning, that I'd forgotten to pull out the little knob, *five.*

✜ *How to Eat an Ice-cream Cone*

BEFORE YOU EVEN GET THE CONE, YOU HAVE TO DO A LOT of planning about it. We'll assume that you lost the argument in the car and that the family has decided to break the automobile journey and stop at an ice-cream stand for cones. Get things straight with them right from the start. Tell them that after they have their cones there will be an imaginary circle six feet away from the car, and that no one—man, woman, or especially child—will be allowed to cross the line and reenter the car until his ice-cream cone has been entirely consumed and he has cleaned himself up. Emphasize: Automobiles and ice-cream cones don't mix. Explain: Melted ice cream, children, is a fluid which is eternally sticky. One drop of it on a car-door handle spreads to the seat covers, to trousers, and thence to hands, and then to the steering wheel, the gear shift, the rear-view mirror, all the knobs of the dashboard—spreads everywhere and lasts forever, spreads from a nice old car like this, which might have to be abandoned because of stickiness, right into a nasty new car, in secret ways that even scientists don't understand. If necessary, even make a joke: "The family that eats ice-cream cones together, sticks together." Then let their mother explain the joke and tell them you don't mean half of what you say, and no, we won't be getting a new car.

Blessed are the children who always eat the same flavor of ice cream or always know beforehand what kind they will want. Such good children should be quarantined from those who say "I want to wait and see what flavors there are." It's hard to just listen, while a beautiful young child who has always been perfectly happy with a plain vanilla ice-cream cone is subverted by a young schoolmate who has been invited along for the weekend, a pleasant and polite child, perhaps, but spoiled by permissive parents and flawed by an overactive imagination. This schoolmate has a flair for contingency planning: "Well, I'll have banana, if they have banana, but if they don't have banana, then I'll have peach, if it's fresh peach, and if they don't have banana or fresh peach, I'll see what else they have that's like that, like maybe fresh strawberry or something, and if they don't have that or anything like that that's good, I'll just have chocolate marshmallow chip or chocolate ripple or something like that." Then—turning to one's own once simple and innocent child, now already corrupt and thinking fast—the schoolmate invites a similar rigmarole: "What kind are *you* going to have?"

I'm a great believer in contingency planning. But none of this is realistic. Few adults, and even fewer children, are able to make up their mind beforehand what kind of ice-cream cone they'll want. It would be nice if they could be all lined up in front of the man who's making up the cones and just snap smartly, when their turn came, "Strawberry, please," "Vanilla, please," "Chocolate, please." But of course it never happens like that. There is always a great discussion, a great jostling and craning of necks and leaning over the counter to see down into the tubs of ice cream, and much intrapersonal consultation—"What kind are *you* having?"—back and forth, as if that should make any difference. Until finally the first child's turn comes and he asks the man, "What kinds do you have?"

Now this is the stupidest question in the world, because there is always a sign posted saying what kinds of ice cream they have. As I tell the children, that's what they put the sign up there for, so you won't have to ask what kinds of ice cream they have. The man gets sick of telling everybody all the different kinds of ice cream they have, so they put a sign up there that says. You're supposed to read it, not ask the man.

"All right, but the sign doesn't say strawberry."

"Well, that means they don't have strawberry."

"But there *is* strawberry, right there."

"That must be raspberry or something." (Look again at the sign. Raspberry isn't there either.)

When the child's turn actually comes, he says, "Do you have strawberry?"

"Sure."

"What other kinds do you have?"

The trouble is, of course, that they put up the sign that says what flavors they have, with little cardboard inserts to put in or take out flavors, way back when they first opened the store. But they never change the sign— or not often enough. They always have flavors that aren't on the list, and often they don't have flavors that *are* on the list. Children know this—whether innately or from earliest experience it would be hard to say. The ice-cream man knows it too. Even grown-ups learn it eventually. There will always be chaos and confusion and mind-changing and general uproar when ice-cream cones are being ordered, and there has not been, is not, and will never be any way to avoid it.

Humans are incorrigibly restless and dissatisfied, always in search of new experiences and sensations, seldom content with the familiar. It is this, I think, that accounts for others wanting to have a taste of your cone, and wanting you to have a taste of theirs. "Do have a taste of this fresh peach, it's delicious," my wife used to say to me, very much (I suppose) the way Eve wanted Adam to taste her delicious apple. An insinuating look of calculating curiosity would film my wife's eyes—the same look those beautiful, scary women in those depraved Italian films give a man they're interested in. "How's *yours?*" she would say. For this reason, I always order chocolate chip now. Down through the years, all those close enough to me to feel entitled to ask for a taste of my cone—namely my wife and step-children—have learned what chocolate chip tastes like, so they have no legitimate reason to ask me for a taste. As for tasting other people's cones, never do it. The reasoning here is that if it tastes good, you'll wish you'd had it; if it tastes bad, you'll have had a taste of something that tastes bad; if it doesn't taste either good or bad, then you won't have missed anything. Of course no person in his right mind ever *would* want to taste anyone else's cone, but it is useful to have good, logical reasons for hating the thought of it.

Another important thing. Never let the man hand you

the ice-cream cones for the whole group. There is no sight more pathetic than some bumbling, disorganized papa holding four ice-cream cones in two hands, with his money still in his pocket, when the man says, "Eighty cents." What does he do then? He can't hand the cones back to the man to hold while he fishes in his pocket for the money, for the man has just given them to *him*. He can start passing them out to the kids, but at least one of them will have gone to the car to see how the dog is doing or have been sent in back by his mother to wash his hands or something. And even if Papa does get them distributed, he's still going to be left with his own cone in one hand, while he tries to get his money with the other. Meanwhile, of course, the man is very impatient, the next group asking him: "What flavors do you have?"

No, never let the man hand you the cones of others. Make him hand each one to each kid individually. That way, too, you won't get disconcerting tastes of butter pecan and black raspberry on your own chocolate chip. And insist that he tell you how much it all costs and settle with him *before* he hands you your own cone. Make sure everyone has got paper napkins and everything *before* he hands you your own cone. Get *everything* straight before he hands you your own cone.

Then, when the moment finally comes, reach out and take it from him. Strange, magical, *dangerous* moment! Consider what it is that you are about to be handed: It is a huge irregular mass of ice cream, faintly domed at the top from the metal scoop which dug it out and then insecurely perched it on the uneven top edge of a hollow inverted cone made out of the most brittle and fragile of materials. Clumps of ice cream hang over the side, very loosely attached to the main body. There is always much more ice cream than the cone could hold, even if the ice cream were tamped down into the cone, which of course it isn't. And the essence of ice cream is that it melts. It doesn't just stay there teetering in this irregular, top-heavy mass, it also *melts*. And it melts fast. And it doesn't just melt, it melts into a stickiness that cannot be wiped off. The only thing one person could hand to another that might possibly be more dangerous is a live hand grenade on which the pin had been pulled five seconds earlier. And of course if anybody offered you that, you could say, "Oh. Uh, well—no thanks."

Ice-cream men handle cones routinely, and are inured. They are like professionals who are used to handling sticks of TNT; their movements quick and skillful. An ice-cream man may attempt to pass a cone to you casually, almost carelessly. Never accept a cone on this basis! Keep your hand at your side, overcoming the instinct by which everyone's hand goes out—almost automatically—whenever he is proffered something delicious and expected. The ice-cream man will look up at you, startled, questioning. Lock his eyes with your own, and *then*, slowly, calmly, and above all, deliberately, take the cone from him.

Grasp the cone firmly but gently between thumb and forefinger, two thirds of the way up. Then dart swiftly away to an open area, away from the jostling crowd at the stand. Then take up the classic ice-cream-cone-eating stance: feet from one to two feet apart, body bent forward from the waist at a twenty-five-degree angle, right elbow well up, right forearm horizontal, at a level with your collarbone and about twelve inches from it. But don't start eating yet! Check first to see what emergency repairs may be necessary. Sometimes a sugar cone will be so crushed or broken or cracked that all you can do is gulp at the thing like a savage, getting what you can of it, as you look frantically around for a trash basket.

Sometimes, of course, a cracked cone can be brought through—but this takes nerve as well as skill. Checking the cone for possible trouble can be done in a second or two, if one knows where to look and does it systematically. A trouble spot some people overlook is the bottom tip of the cone. This may have been broken off. Or the flap of the cone material at the bottom, usually wrapped over itself in that funny spiral construction, may be folded in a way that is imperfect and leaves an opening. No need to say that through this opening—in a matter of perhaps thirty or at most ninety seconds—will begin to pour hundreds of thousands of atoms of sticky melted ice cream. In this case you must instantly get the paper napkin in your left hand under the bottom of the cone to stem the forthcoming flow, or be doomed to eat the cone far too rapidly. It is a grim moment. No one wants to eat a cone under that kind of pressure, but neither does he want to end up with the bottom of the cone stuck to a messy napkin. There's an alternative, one that takes both skill and courage: Forgoing any cradling of the cone, grasp it more firmly between thumb and forefinger and extend the other fingers so that they are out of the way of the dripping from the bottom; then increase the waist-bend angle from twenty-five degrees to thirty-five degrees, and then eat the cone, *allowing* it to drip out of the bottom onto the ground in front of you! Experienced and thoughtful cone-eaters acclaim the successful execution of this dangerous acceptance of the broken-tip challenge.

So far, we have been discussing irregularities in the cone itself. But of course there is the ice cream to worry about too. In this area immediate action is sometimes needed on three fronts at once. Frequently the ice cream will be mounted on the cone in a way that is perilously lopsided. This requires immediate corrective action to move it back into balance—a slight pressure downward with the teeth and lips to seat the ice cream more firmly in and on the cone—but not so hard, of course, as to break the cone. On other occasions, gobs of ice cream will be hanging loosely from the main body, about to fall to the ground (bad) or onto one's hand (far, far worse). This requires instant action too: snapping at the gobs with the split-second timing of a frog in a swarm of flies. But sometimes trickles of ice cream will already (already!) be running down the cone toward one's fingers, and one must quickly raise the cone, tilting one's face skyward, and lick with an upward motion to push the trickles away from the fingers and (as much as possible) into the mouth.

Which to do first? Every ice-cream cone is like every other ice-cream cone in that it has the potential to present all three problems, but each ice-cream cone is paradoxically unique in that it will present the problems in a different order of emergency, and hence require a different order of solutions. And it is (thank God!) an unusual ice-cream cone that will present all three problems in *exactly* the same degree of emergency. It is necessary to make an instantaneous judgment as to where the greatest danger is, and *act!* The whole thing will be a mess before you've even tasted it. If it isn't possible to decide between any given two of the basic three emergencies—lopsided mount, dangling gobs, already running trickles—then make an arbitrary adjudication: Assign a "heads" value to one and a "tails" value to the other, then flip a coin to decide which is to be tended to first. Don't for heaven's sake, *actually* flip a coin—you'd have to dig in your pockets for it. (Unless you had it ready in your hand before you were handed the cone, in case this sort of problem developed.) There isn't remotely enough time for anything like that. Just decide *in your mind* which came up—heads or tails —and then try to remember as fast as you can which of the problems it was that had been assigned to the winning side of the coin.

In trying to make wise and correct decisions about the ice-cream cone in your hand, you should always try to keep your ultimate objective in mind. The first objective is to get the cone under control. Secondarily, one will want to eat the cone calmly and with pleasure. Real pleasure, of course, lies not simply in enjoying the taste of the ice-cream cone, but in eating it *right,* which is where the ultimate objective comes in.

Let us assume that you have darted to your open space and made your necessary emergency repairs. The cone is still dangerous, of course—still, so to speak, "live." But you can now proceed with it in an orderly fashion. First revolve the cone through the full 360 degrees, turning the cone by moving the thumb away from you and the fore finger toward you, so the cone moves counterclockwise. Snap at the loose gobs of ice cream as you do this. Then, with the cone still "wound," which will require the wrist to be bent at the full right angle toward you, apply pressure with the mouth and tongue to accomplish overall realignment, straightening and settling the whole mess. Then, unwinding the cone back through the full 360 degrees, remove any trickles of ice cream. Now, have a look at the cone. Some supplementary repairs may be necessary, but the cone is now defused.

At this point, you can risk a glance around you to see how badly the others are doing with their cones. Then, shaking your head with good-natured contempt for the mess they're making, you can settle down to eating yours. This is done by eating the ice cream off the top, at each bite pressing down cautiously, so that the ice cream settles farther and farther into the cone, being very careful not to break the cone. Of course, you never take so much ice cream into your mouth at once that it hurts your teeth; and for the same reason never let unmelted ice cream into the back of your mouth. If these procedures are followed correctly, you should shortly arrive at the ideal, your ultimate objective, the way an ice-cream cone is always pictured as being, but never actually is when it is handed to you. The ice cream should now form a small dome whose large circumference exactly coincides with the large circumference of the cone itself: a small skullcap that fits exactly on top of a larger, inverted dunce cap.

Like the artist, who makes order out of chaos, you have taken an unnatural, abhorrent, irregular, chaotic form like this: and from it you have sculpted an ordered, ideal shape that might be envied by Praxiteles or even Euclid:

Now at last you can begin to take little nibbles of the cone itself, being very careful not to crack it. Revolve the cone so that its rim remains level as it descends, while you eat both ice cream and cone. Because it is in the geometrical nature of things, the inverted cone shape, as you keep nibbling the top off it, still remains a cone *shape;* and because you are constantly reforming with your tongue the little dome of ice cream on top, it follows in logic—and in actual practice, if you are skillful and careful—that as you eat the cone on down it continues to look exactly the same, so that at the very end you will hold between your thumb and forefinger a tiny, idealized replica of an ice-cream cone, a harmless thing perhaps an inch high.

Then, while the others are licking their sticky fingers, preparatory to wiping them on their clothes, or going back to the ice-cream stand for more paper napkins to try to clean themselves up—*then* you can hold the miniature cone up for everyone to see, and pop it gently into your mouth.

❀ How to Care
for and About Ashtrays

THERE ARE THREE TRUTHS ABOUT ASHTRAYS THAT MUST BE held self-evident before any household can achieve true happiness and security: (1) there can never really ever be too many ashtrays, because (2) there must be an ashtray, a specific ashtray, for each and every place anyone could conceivably ever want one, and (3) it must *be* there—always. No ashtray should ever be moved.

But there are forces at work against order in the world. The natural enemies of the ashtray are wives and children. Children are always putting something else in ashtrays: wadded Kleenex, pear cores, gum and gum wrappers, orange peels. And this of course means that wives take the ashtrays off to the kitchen, intending to wash them, which isn't the right way to clean ashtrays anyway, but then just leave them in the sink.

To clean ashtrays the right way, proceed as follows. Take a metal or plastic or wooden (but never a basket) wastebasket in your left hand, and a paper towel in your right. Approach the ashtray that is to be cleaned. Put the wastebasket down on the floor, and with your released left hand pick up the ashtray and dump its contents of cigarette ends, spent matches, and loose ashes (nothing else should be in an ashtray!) into the wastebasket. Then, still holding the ashtray over the basket, rub gently with the paper towel at any of the few stains or spots that may remain. Then put the ashtray carefully back into its place, pick up the wastebasket again, and approach the next ashtray to be cleaned. It should never be necessary to wash an ashtray, if it is kept clean and dry. Throughout its whole lifetime in a well-ordered household, an ashtray need never travel more than three feet from where it belongs, and never be out of place at all for more than thirty seconds.

But when children put pear cores and orange peels in ashtrays, of course none of this can be accomplished as it ought. One can't dump raw garbage into a wastepaper basket and then calmly put the basket back in the corner of the room. And the juice of the fruit moistens the ashtray so ashes stick and dry in hard spots so it may *need* to be washed. Then the ashtrays get left in the kitchen to drain dry, because no one likes to use a dishtowel to dry an ashtray. And then there's no ashtray where it's supposed to be when you want it, so you have to move one from somewhere else and gradually everything gets all upset and things in the household aren't the way they ought to be, even though it's not your fault.

❀ How to Cut Down on Smoking and Drinking Quite So Much

THE TROUBLE WITH MOST ADVICE YOU GET ABOUT SMOKING and drinking is that it comes from the wrong people. It's the strange people who have somehow managed to quit smoking entirely who are only too willing to tell you how they did it and how you ought to too. It's the ex-alcoholics who couldn't handle booze at all who are always trying to tell you you have to give it up entirely. Their solution is worse than your problem. You don't want to *stop* smoking and drinking, you just want to stop smoking and drinking *so much.*

And it's true, probably, that if you were able to smoke and drink less, you'd actually enjoy it *more.* On those days when you run through two or three packs of cigarettes, you don't really even notice them, just putting them out and lighting them up more or less automatically. The same is of course true of the third or fourth martini: you don't even taste it, it might as well be water. But it's not, oh God, it's not. And all this leads to hangovers—real hangovers and cigarette hangovers too.

Cutting down is a good idea, too, because it's the best way of assuring that you won't have to stop. No one wants to have to give up drinking. And take it from me, you might as well not even *try* to give up smoking. All you'll do is make a nightmare for yourself, your family, and your colleagues, for four days or four weeks or four months, depending on how long you manage to last. People who claim to have quit were always latently non-smokers or they wouldn't be able to function. But *you'd* never feel quite right without it: there'd always be the sense that something's missing in your life, and you'd come back to it sooner or later. So why torture yourself? Lung cancer is a terrible thing (my father died of it), and early death from emphysema or heart trouble doesn't sound too good either, but a life without cigarettes may be like what the Greeks said of the unexamined life: it's not worth living.

One good thing about drinking (besides how it makes you feel) is that it is legal and socially acceptable more or less everywhere. In this, it is just about unique—except for sex, which is different—among all the euphoria-producing things, like marijuana or dreadful amylnitrate in the friendly Burroughs-Welcome yellow tin boxes, or all the rest of those scary agents that give you a loss of sense of one's awful self and hence an acute sense of well-being. It is a great enemy of the blues. Drinking is great.

But there's an underestimated aspect to smoking, too, one that's very singular in this dislocated modern society where we're all made restless and anxious by a lot of hidden desires and aimless longings—needs that generally go not just unfulfilled but largely unrecognized. I mean, if you have an unrecognized longing to recapture your lost youth, for instance, it's a need that can't be satisfied by a sexy, powerful, rebellious, new young automobile, no matter what the TV commercials imply—nor by a springtime-fresh cigarette either, for that matter. But what a cigarette *can* satisfy is your need for a cigarette. Longing for a cigarette is one of the least aimless longings there is. Creating thus their own recognizable desire *and* the means of fulfilling it, cigarettes figure as both hunger *and* indulgence, aspiration *and* achievement, lust *and* sensuality, the quest *and* the grail. That the longing is artificially established (an addiction) makes this all the more remarkable.

That cigarettes desert you when you need them most—when you get a cold—is not a material criticism. It is great when they do start tasting good again and you know you are getting over your cold. Several years ago I was bitten three times by two wasps (different pairs of them, of course) about six months apart, each time with a fantastically worse reaction. The next time is supposed to kill me and I carry some sort of adrenalin tablets around with me that I don't have much faith in. I keep wanting to try them, but never have a chance—thank God, I guess. Anyway, the last (third) time I was bitten by two wasps I nearly did die. I thought I'd had a heart attack. Coming finally out of the anaphylactic shock or whatever it's called—believe me, it's like coming back from the dead—well, *coming* back from the dead, the first thing I wanted was my sense of humor back and when I saw I'd got that the next thing I wanted, the *first* thing I wanted after I saw I was alive, was a cigarette. Dr. Haliday, who had rushed over to give me the adrenalin shot that brought me back (since gone to the grave himself), had given up smoking about six months before, but he breathed a great sigh and had a cigarette with me. I mean, if I died of *lung cancer* and then somehow managed to come back to life, what I'd want first is a cigarette. So would you. So would any sensible person.

Imagine a cup of coffee without a cigarette. There'd be no point in it. There'd be no reason to get up in the morning. The main reason for eating a meal is how good a cigarette tastes afterward. Imagine taking a break in your work—for coffee or just for a rest—if you couldn't have a cigarette. There's no point in stopping at all, no point in even *doing* a job, much less doing it *right*, unless when you're through you can reward yourself with a cigarette.

But the "reward" idea is one of our main troubles with smoking and drinking. When the work's going well you think you "deserve" to smoke as much as you want. After a long hard day of good work at the office you deserve to unwind with a few drinks. After a long hard week, you feel you deserve to get drunk on Friday night. All that's true: you do deserve it. But ultimately so much self-rewarding becomes self-punishing. Feeling lousy all weekend is the reward you get for your hard week's work. It doesn't seem fair, I know; and if I were God I'd make it that people would never get hangovers unless they didn't deserve to get drunk. I would do that for you, but I can't.

It also may be that you drink and smoke so much because you like it: you like the feeling that a drink, or a lot of drinks, gives you; and while you may not exactly *like* the feeling a cigarette gives you, you sure as hell *don't* like the feeling you get when you haven't had one for an hour or two; also, you may actually like the taste of tobacco and liquor. But the real reason you drink and smoke so much is that you still have the idea, formed somewhere way back when, that smoking and drinking too much is really a very romantic thing to do. It seems very grown-up to you if you are young, and it seems very youthful to you if you are old.

In his autobiography, Lincoln Steffens describes his romance with drinking:

> Once, for example, as I staggered (a little more than I had to) away from the bar, I overheard one man say to another:
> "Those boys can carry some liquor, can't they?"
> That was great. But better still was the other loafer's reply: "Yes," he said, "but it's tough to see young men setting out on the downgrade to hell that way."

The romantic idea that one has a brilliant future somehow being ruined by drinking is natural to a college sophomore, but it ought to be abandoned in maturity. The trouble is it remains in the subconscious, sneakily invidious, so that even the ugly hangover becomes glamorous. When I was young and seldom got hangovers, or not bad ones, I'd often pretend to be in a very bad way "the morning after." It made for a lot of companionable talk in college about "the hair of the dog" and getting "a quick one." (Experimenting with drugs—which comes complete with that great language about "turning on" and "highs" and "freaked out" and "coming down" and so on—must seem marvelously romantic to students today.) I remember, the first time I did have a hangover, what a feeling of pride I had about it. And years and years later, when the pride was replaced by shame on a number of occasions, when for various reasons I tried to conceal how my hands were trembling, I remember even then having that invidious secret sense of how romantic it was that I was in such a bad way and actually trying to conceal it.

It's in our earliest, most impressionable youth that we learn how romantic it is to be dissolute. I remember how we used to hang around Lou Berry's stationery store in Williston Park endlessly discussing Wilbur Slaymacher, a stunted unattractive kid we all admired because all he ever had for breakfast was a Coke and a coffin nail. Once you have come to the realization that Wilbur Slaymacher, "setting out on the downgrade to hell that way," as Lincoln Steffens puts it, despite the key fact that there was nothing else to recommend him at all, is nevertheless *a genuinely romantic figure*, once you grasp that, in late childhood or early adolescence, it is something (a lesson learned, or something) that you never ever get over. It is with you the rest of your life, this misconception.

Oh, I could tell you other stories about how romantic smoking and drinking are. How, for instance, when I came home from Europe determined to straighten myself out, I went to *Esquire* looking for a job, and there in this big Madison Avenue office were Frederick A. Birmingham, The Editor, and Leonard Wallace Robinson, The Managing Editor, and they were talking dirty and kidding around with Imie Camelli, the secretary, and were real slick and smooth, but easy about it somehow; and then FAB said he had an eleven-thirty appointment with his dentist and then a lunch date with George Frazier or Leslie Saalberg or someone elegant like that, and he and Len got to joking about how when you had a martini after having novocain you could only feel one side of the glass and when you ate the olive you could only taste half of it. It doesn't seem very funny now, but God did it seem marvelous then. I had no job, no apartment, dwindling money, my father was dying of you-know-what and my mother was a real problem, there was a heat wave, I had poison ivy, terrible athlete's foot, bleeding gums from trenchmouth, had just gotten divorced, and for the first (and probably last) time in my life I thought New York City was great. Maybe it was the idea of going to the dentist on office time. Maybe it was the idea of an expense-account lunch. But I think what seemed so romantic and great was having to have your martinis at lunch even though your mouth was shot full of novocain.

Or I could tell about taking my stepson, smoking at age fourteen, to a doctor to give him the big health-scare. Smoking when you have a tendency to asthma is insane: the kid should know it. Well, the doctor tried, telling all about the little end parts of the lung that get clogged up and all, but what he did was make it seem more dangerous and hence more romantic than ever. That afternoon on the tennis courts I overheard enough to realize that the story of The Doctor's Warning had been told around to all the other hot-shot teen-agers. All I'd done was contribute to the creation of a Wilbur Slaymacher figure. The more horrible the facts and statistics that come out about smoking, the more attractive it seems to be to a certain kind of normal irrational adolescent mentality—that is, most of the kids and virtually all the adults I know.

One of the ways to cut down is to work a kind of jujitsu on this crazy secret conviction. Get it in your mind that cutting down is really *just* as romantic. Instead of confessing (really boasting) about how much you drink and smoke, confess-boast about how much you *used* to drink and smoke. "Boy, I *had* to cut down," you can say. "I was slowly killing myself."

Then tell how the other day you'd found your hands trembling and you'd tried to *conceal* it, and how that shook you up. How you calculated just how much you had to drink a day, and how that shook you up too. "It was damn near a fifth," you say. "Two or three drinks at lunch, three before dinner, then go to a party, or just have a couple of nightcaps at home. It all adds up. Figure it out." Then explain how many cigarettes you smoked: "I was up to damn near three packs a day. My heart would pound with this crazy rhythm, and my chest was so constricted I thought there was a steel band running around it playing some kind of weird calypso death march."

Don't actually say all these things to people, of course; you'll bore them, and they'll blame me. No one's interested in listening to you run on about how and why you're cutting down. If the other person's cutting down himself, he wants to tell you; if he isn't, he doesn't want to hear how he ought to. The things I'm telling you to say are just the kinds of things you *imagine* yourself saying as a way of coming to terms with something that's happened to you or a new idea you've got about yourself.

The actual methods you use to cut down aren't as important as getting your mind right about it. The basic idea is that you limit yourself in certain specific arbitrary ways. For instance, note the times in a day when you really enjoy a cigarette and stick to those times. Or keep a pad of paper next to the package and write down the time you take a smoke; this just helps you to keep track so that you don't get to smoking wildly. Or decide you'll have one cigarette each hour—at ten minutes after each hour, for instance—and check your watch before lighting up. Or keep the cigarettes somewhere where you'll have to get up each time you want one. It's a nuisance, but that's the *point* of it.

Or, you can set a limit on how many you'll smoke each day—say ten or fifteen or even thirty—and count them out each morning into the elegant silver case you got from your grandfather or a junk store. To stick to just one package of twenty per day is difficult because the pack is right there in your pocket the way it always is and you reach in and take one and smoke it without thinking and then one of your cigarettes for the day is gone and that makes you mad and you tend to go off the whole deal. So put a piece of Scotch tape over the refolded top of the package and before you take out a cigarette you'll remember what you're doing. One package a day is not too hard: you can get through the morning on four; smoke six in the afternoon; then you still have ten left for the evening, when the will is weaker. If you're using a system like this, you need a real cigarette like a Camel so that you can appreciate it and have it satisfy you. Now that you're smoking so much less, there's no need for healthful, tasteless filter brands or the disgusting crème-de-menthe kind that supposedly refresh your taste with menthol. When you first go onto one-pack-a-day, though, get long cigarettes like Pall Malls; you can always cut them in half if it looks as though you're running ahead of yourself in the middle of the

97

afternoon. The system gets thrown off when someone disastrously bums a cigarette from you, but then there's joy when someone offers you one of his, an extra you don't have to count. As a regular smoker I'm indulgent to people who try to cut down by bumming instead of buying, but not everyone is. And I just stand in awe of those who are able to cut down by not starting smoking until some fixed hour, say noon or 5 P.M.

A scheme that worked awhile for me not long ago was writing down a *reason* for every cigarette I had: "work break," "before lunch," "after lunch," "need to reconsider what done so far," and so on. After a few days the reasons tended to get arbitrary ("sheer hell of it") or indulgent, ("I want it"), and even sentimental ("this one's for our boys in Vietnam"). When I found myself writing down ten reasons *in advance* one afternoon so that I could just go ahead and smoke whenever I wanted, I gave the system up.

All these systems eventually break down: that may be in the nature of using system as a process of personal reform. You're interested in the system for a while; then you get impatient with it. The thing to do then is switch to another. I'll admit a system isn't much of a *system* when you're switching from one to another all the time. But it's what you have to do, all you *can* do.

I had one hell of a system once for cutting down on drinking so much. We were sharing a big summer house with a lot of city people, and I came to realize I'd been getting bombed every night. It was another of the times I'd more or less quit working, and I was there all the time; the others would come up just weekends or on their vacations. Anyway, I devised this incredibly clever system: the idea was, I'd plan ahead just exactly what I would do drinking-wise for each and every day of a four-day cycle. On what became known as A First Day, I wouldn't drink at all—nothing, not a single drink. This was to prove I wasn't an alcoholic and could do without it. On the next day, A Second Day, I would have one drink before dinner and one drink after dinner—that's all, no more, no matter how often they told me I was a no-fun person. This was to prove I wasn't an alcoholic and could drink abstemiously, if that isn't a contradiction in terms. On A Third Day, I'd allow myself to drink what I called "moderately." This was to prove I could drink moderately. And on A Fourth Day, it was all-out, anything goes, as much as I wanted. This was to prove I was still a fun person. Then it would be A First Day again. And so on.

Well, the system really did sort of work for a while, but there were difficulties with it, as I guess you must have imagined there would be. On A First Day, after A Fourth Day debauch, is of course just when you need a drink most, at least one drink, if not just one drink before dinner then at least one drink just before bed. On A First Day I'd be irascible all day and go to bed early and not be able to sleep. A Second Day was all right, nothing to get excited about, but the way sensible people live regularly, I guess. A Third Day was always a problem, because my idea of "moderately" kept changing as the evening wore on. A Fourth Day, of course, was just the normal disaster.

One of the main problems of the system was the four-day cycle when everyone else was more or less on a seven-day week. I can't for the life of me now remember how I decided on four days or why on earth I didn't change when I saw it wasn't working. If my Fourth Day were to come, say, on the others' Tuesday, there wouldn't be anyone to drink with me; it was awful having A Fourth Day go to waste like that. Then, others couldn't keep track of what day mine was. They'd prolong the cocktail hour unconscionably on A Second Day that happened to be their Friday night. Or I'd be moderately having a couple of drinks on A Third Day, maybe weaving a little as I told a long-winded story (you know how I am), maybe making myself one more at the same time, and I'd overhear one of the householders ask another, "Say, is this A Fourth Day, or what?"

Toward the end, I began switching my days around to accommodate, like a good householder, so *my* good days would coincide with *their* good days. Like on A Second Day Saturday night, I'd decide during cocktails to have my Second Day tomorrow and my Third Day today; then later in the evening I'd decide to make today my Fourth Day and have my Third Day tomorrow and have my Second Day after that. But things tended to get confused, and of course the First and Second Days got kind of lost, and pretty soon every day was A Fourth Day again. It's really hard to organize systems when you're sharing with others.

But good planning is still really the central secret in cutting down. Good planning and careful scheduling can solve most of Life's so-called Problems. You just have to get control of your life. You are *bound* to have too much to drink and too many cigarettes if you have to wait for someone in a restaurant, not knowing what to do with your hands and wondering whether people are wondering why you're waiting there. It's not your fault in cases like this. You don't so much *get* drunk, as you get *taken* drunk.

Hostesses know this. It's the company they don't think is going to get along too well, the meal they're not sure is good enough, that's the kind of thing they try to cover up by letting cocktails run from seven until ten. By then everyone is smashed, and even though they're arguing viciously they think they're having a good time. Probably everyone will look back on it as a "memorable" evening. A memorable evening, almost by definition (some kind of weird paradoxical definition), is usually one you don't remember terribly clearly. Your whole next day (or two) is destroyed by this woman so that she can make her disaster of a party seem like a success. What's happened is that you've allowed yourself to be victimized by someone else's inadequacy. You've even collaborated in your own victimization, which makes it worse.

Good planning, on the other hand, features (or *would* feature, if one could ever work things out right) each cigarette and each drink as a pleasant event occurring routinely in the course of a well-ordered day. You would have your first cigarette with your second cup of coffee after you've finished your breakfast at precisely 8:07, in the middle of the CBS World News Round-up. You would have your second precisely at 10:15, when you took your coffee break, *after* you've got your milk and sugar in the coffee and tasted it and it's just right and everything is set for full enjoyment. Then if you take a glass of sherry before lunch at 12:30 you have another cigarette then. And so on, through a prescheduled, *ordered* day. If you can basically keep to a schedule like this, then you can afford to, indeed you deserve to, go off the schedule on special occasions.

Drinking to a schedule presents some of the same hazards and delights as smoking a definite, limited number of cigarettes each day. You have to get everything all set and ready so that you realize both that you're having your drink and also that you're appreciating it. Sometimes you forget, or get busy doing something else, or you're talking with somebody, and you forget you're having your drink, and you just drink it down, and then you've drunk it and didn't even realize you were having it, must less appreciate it, and that makes you feel as if you'd been cheated out of it, so you want to have another right away to make up for it, and that's bad.

So there should be a sense of occasion for having your drinks. I don't for heaven's sake mean a party or anything like that. There's nothing worse than a party for making you forget you're having your drink! No, I mean like a particular time of day to have it, or them. How many drinks a day are you going to allow yourself? Three? Five? If you are going to have five you certainly don't want to bunch them or you'll find yourself having ten. If you're only having two or three you'll want to make them good big strong ones with some punch to them, so you'll *know* you're having them. Nice brown drinks. Certainly you'll want one, or two, before dinner. Maybe you'll want one before lunch, or a glass of wine with lunch (counts one half); and maybe you like to take a nice scotch on the rocks upstairs to bed with you? Fine. You can have anything you want—as long as you don't want everything else too, of course.

Now a good way of creating this sense of occasion

about drinks is to have a different kind of drink for each of the different occasions. I mean, if you go through life never having anything but Johnnie Walker Red Label and water, the only difference between your drinks is the time of day you have them. My parents always had, every night before dinner, either a martini or a manhattan. "Which did we have last night?" one of them would say, and then, "Well, let's have the other, then," or "Oh, let's have it again tonight anyway." A manhattan is a much underrated drink: it *is* kind of sticky and you certainly wouldn't want it every night or even every other night; but it is a cheerful drink, and if it is cold and bleak (the weather, I mean) and you wish you had an open fire, a manhattan is good, perhaps because the cherry in it has some of the same bright warm color. Martinis give you a headache, as everyone knows; but made in a good expensive restaurant there is nothing like them. One martini is all one ever allows oneself to have, of course; unless the other person has three, in which case you can have two.

Unlike the martini, which should be drunk out, the whiskey sour can only be drunk at home. They are simple to make: juice of one half lemon, one teaspoon superfine sugar, two ounces American whiskey, shake vigorously but elegantly. But even your best bars are not set up to squeeze fresh individual lemon juice. The other great drink to make at home is the negroni. *Very* easy: one ounce of good fragrant gin, one ounce of Italian vermouth, one ounce of Campari; stir it up with a lot of ice and pour it into a chilled stemmed cocktail glass and then take an orange peel and bend and twist it so that the oil from the peel squirts all over the top of the drink. Oh, delicious.

Most liqueurs are terrible, of course, and haven't enough kick in them to be worth wasting one of your drinks on. Brandy (cognac) gives you heartburn and is fiery and antagonistic and makes you thirsty and one leads to another. The other liqueurs are like dessert— crème de cacao, Grand Marnier, and those. But anis is real great. I mean anis, not anisette; and Anis del Mono is better than Anis de Gorilla, if you are ever faced with the choice; and there was a kind of anis they had at the Spanish Pavilion at the New York World's Fair in 1962 or 1963 I think it was, that was even better than Anis del Mono or any anis they ever had in Spain so far as I know. God knows what it was called: if you could figure out how to write them you could ask them.

There are lots of other drinks that are good, mostly the classic ones carefully made, rather than new concoctions the distillers think up. The best pernod-type drink by me is the Ricard *pastis,* but that's best to drink in the south of France or on Guadalupe or somewhere, where it gets to be sort of habit-forming, like smoking Gauloises. Then there's rum and ginger beer, which you make with a light, cheap rum because the imported ginger beer costs so much; it's great coming back into the harbor after a day-sail, or even after tennis, especially in August, when you feel you can't drink another gin and tonic you're so fed up with them. With margaritas, it's kind of a bind keeping the tequila and triple sec in stock, and tequila blows the mind and numbs the legs if you have too many; but it's great fun fussing to get the salt arranged on the rim of the glass just right, and they surely are delicious. Say, what *time* is it getting to be?!

Anyway, my theory is that if you enjoy your drinks

you won't want so many of them. What gets you drunk is thinking that subsequent drinks are going to pick you up the way the first one did, but of course it doesn't work that way. Another theory I have is that the best drinks always taste faintly medicinal. They either taste sort of cough-syrupy-medicinal like the manhattan or a good cream sherry or the rum and ginger beer, or they taste sort of antiseptic-medicinal like the martini or the gin and tonic or the scotch and soda. Why the negroni is so great is it tastes *both* syrupy and antiseptic, bitter *and* sweet. Whiskey sours and rum drinks practically *are* medicine, full of good-for-you lemon juice with vitamin C. Now as to *why* the best drinks always taste somehow medicinal, as to why one would *want* his drinks to taste like medicine, I have another theory. It ties in with the romance-of-drinking business: the reason drinking seems so romantic to us, us middle-class, middle-aged Americans, is that it seems so *wrong*. It is a *very naughty* thing to be doing, drinking. I don't know whether this is an historically inherited coast-to-coast Puritan hangup or an acquired-from-childhood individual-by-individual hangup. The fact remains that the best-tasting drinks taste like medicine, and I find the implications of that difficult to take and hard to swallow. In fact, the more I scratch at the surface of the middle-class, middle-aged American male's motivations about drinking and smoking (this one's at least), the less I like what I see.

It may really be that routines, schedules, systems, and the general imposition of order on one's self and one's life are ultimately no match for the tendencies toward indulgence, excess, and chaos that are abroad in the land

and apparently inherent within. But you do see, don't you, that all the things I've been telling you hang together? An ordered system-schedule *ought* to work, God knows. It takes fully into account your first realization about smoking and drinking—that you feel you "deserve" a drink or smoke as a "reward." And the method accounts for—in fact, utilizes—your second realization—that you think smoking and drinking are romantic—for this is a truly grown-up way to drink and smoke. You've got to begin thinking of yourself as a mature, organized adult, not as some talented but tragically flawed kid, harum-scarum and hell-bent. That's not you, not any more—and besides, you "had" to resort to this system because things were really getting out of control and you were headed downhill fast. And your third realization—that the ordered, scheduled life ultimately provides more pleasure (I realize you haven't really *realized* this yet)—will be manifest in the relish with which you appreciate each cigarette and each drink as it becomes available to you in the time-scheme you set up. Then, there's also the fun of anticipating them. It's perhaps needless to say that *considerable* anticipation can develop by the time to have the next cigarette or drink comes around. But awful as the waiting is, it's better than giving them up.

❈ *How to Do Four Dumb Tricks with a Package of Camels*

ANOTHER REASON FOR SMOKING CAMELS, BESIDES BECAUSE they satisfy, never change, are available most everywhere, are romantically-dangerously unfiltered, and taste best, is that there are four dumb tricks you can do with the package that amuse children and other simple-minded amiable people.

You need a certain amount of equipment. First and foremost you need a package of Camels, like this:

Second, you will need a small mirror. Third, a dime. And fourth, a child or reasonable fascimile.

DUMB TRICK NUMBER ONE

Show the front of the package, which shows the camel standing there in the desert. Ask the child: "If a sandstorm came up, where would you go?"

CHILD: "Into the pyramid?"

YOU: "No."

CHILD: "Up the palm tree?"

YOU: "No, that wouldn't protect you from a sandstorm."

CHILD (finally): "I give up."

You turn the package over and say, "To this city on the other side."

DUMB TRICK NUMBER TWO

Show the front of the package again and give the child the dime. Say: "Cover the four legs of the camel with the dime." The child tries, the dime won't quite cover them all.

CHILD: "Can I use two nickels? Is that the trick?"

YOU: "No, it has to be a dime."

CHILD: "Well, can I use *one* nickel?"

YOU: "No. I just said it has to be a dime. The whole point of it is to try to do it with a dime."

CHILD: "Well, a dime won't cover all four legs."

YOU: "Do you give up?"

CHILD: "Let me try some more. There must be some trick to it."

YOU: "Of course there's a trick to it. That's the point.

I told you I'd show you four dumb tricks to do with a package of Camels."

CHILD: "Well, I give up."

You take the dime and cover the *fore*feet of the camel.

CHILD: "You said to cover all four legs!"

YOU: "I said '*the* forelegs.' These *are* the forelegs, the two front legs."

CHILD: "Oh, I get it. That's dumb, though. What's the next one?"

DUMB TRICK NUMBER THREE

YOU: "Find the Arabic writing on the Camel package."
Child takes package and looks all over it.

YOU (encouragingly): "There must be some. It's Turkish tobacco."

CHILD: "Well, where is it? I don't see any Arabic writing. What's it look like?"

YOU: "Do you give up?"

CHILD: "Is it on the pyramid or on one of the towers on the back?"

YOU: "No, there isn't any there. You don't see any there, do you?"

CHILD: "No. But maybe it's there, very small or something." Child looks at the mirror. "Maybe if I had a magnifying glass . . . What's the mirror for?"

YOU: "Never mind the mirror. Do you give up?"

CHILD: "I guess so."

You take the mirror and hold it so that the edge of the package that says "CHOICE QUALITY" in big letters is reflected in it, holding your finger over it so that the child sees only the reflection. For some reason known only to God and maybe a few physicists, the "CHOICE" is reflected perfectly well, but the "QUALITY" goes completely to pieces and looks very Arabic, thus:

CHOICE ÓNAΓIΓY

CHILD: "That does look like Arabic. But why does the 'CHOICE' stay the same way?"

YOU: "It's very mysterious. Only a few physicists understand it."

CHILD: "That's better than the other ones anyway. What's the next one?"

YOU: "The *last* one, not the next one."

DUMB TRICK NUMBER FOUR

This is the worst and dumbest one of all. You say to the child: "Find the date '1914' on the package." The child looks and looks and looks. The child has been tricked three times now and really wants to guess this one.

CHILD: "It's really there?"

YOU: "Yes."

CHILD: "It's really *there?* I mean, it's not outside the package or something?"

YOU: "What do you mean by that?"

CHILD: "I don't know. It's really *on* the package, *written* there, the date '1914'?"

YOU (in a hedging tone): "Yes, more or less. The date '1914' is written there on the package."

CHILD (looking at the mirror): "Is it backward or anything?"

YOU: "Well, it may be backward and it may not. Anyway, you don't need the mirror."

CHILD: "What do you mean it's backward and I don't need the mirror?"

YOU: "I didn't say it *was* backward."

CHILD: "Well, *is* it backward?"

YOU: "I'm not saying any more. Do you give up?"

CHILD (musing): "It's *on* the package and it *may* be backward. It's some kind of trick, isn't it?"

YOU: "Of course it's a trick. These are all tricks."

CHILD: "But it's *there?*"

YOU: "Yes, for heaven's sake. Do you give up?"

Now it's important on this one that the child does give up, really gives up, is even finally put in the position of begging you to show him, because it's an especially dumb trick and he's going to be disappointed when he's shown the "1914." On the back of the package, left over for some reason from some copywriter's bright idea twenty or thirty years ago when most cigarette makers gave out gift coupons is this message:

Don't look for premiums or
coupons, as the cost of
the tobaccos blended in
CAMEL Cigarettes pro-
hibits the use of them.

And upside-down and backward, of course, the "hibi" in "prohibits" reads "1914"—sort of.

CHILD: "Ugh."

YOU: "I know three more, but I won't show you."

How to Daydream

Daydreaming is something you've got to do on your own to a very substantial extent. I mean, I'm interested in telling you how to do things right, but it wouldn't *be* right, would it, if I told you what to daydream, and then you just went ahead and daydreamed that, out of ineptitude or sheer laziness? The whole point of daydreaming is to have it be about what you want, and it's a waste of time, anyway: you start daydreaming about what someone else wants, you'll *really* be wasting your time. Still, I *can* show you *how* it's done.

You should develop some special overall method, then work up specific material from areas you know something about. Because I more or less dropped out of what's called "the world" in more or less early middle age, what I daydream about best is getting back into it in some big-deal way. And because what I used to be "in" was publishing, a lot of my daydreams have to do with that—but not all of them, not by any means. The basic technique I use is that *"they" come to me*. They come to get me out of retirement because they realize that I'm the only man who can do whatever it is they want done right. This utilizes a lot of my best stuff.

I SAVE *LIFE*

For instance, a daydream I find pleasant and useful is that Hedley Donovan or James Linen or whoever those people are who run the Time-Life organization—at any rate, "they"—come to me and say: "Rust—you don't mind if we call you 'Rust,' do you?—Rust, I don't know if you've got wind of it up here, but we're in trouble with *Life:* advertising's soft and circulation's expensive. Television news has sapped the vitality of the photojournalism we used to do so well, and there's a feeling the magazine has lost its rationale. Casting about for a new concept, we've come up with what we think is one hell of a good idea: if we can find the right editor for it, we're ready to switch *Life* over to run nothing but fiction. We believe serious literary fiction has a very great deal to tell us about how we live now in this country, and someone told us you do too. You could pay absolutely top rates, have three or four major novels running in serial simultaneously, eight or ten stories by Famous Name Writers and Promising Young Writers, plus a couple of novellas, *each week.* You can imagine how a market like this would revitalize the American novel and short story! We'd handle all the business stuff; you'd have a completely free hand editorially; make your own hours and choose your own staff, of course. You'd start at fifty grand, but there are a lot of fringe benefits at Time-Life; and if the magazine makes the kind of comeback we think it will in your hands, you'd be up to around a hundred thousand in no time. You don't want to see *Life* go the way of *Collier's*, the *Post* and *Look*, do you? We've looked the whole field over, Rust; we'll level with you about that. But you're the one we're coming to first. We've come to you because you are the only magazine fiction editor who can do this thing *right*. You interested at all?"

I WOW THEM WITH MY IDEAS
FOR A TV SHOW

Or they come to me in the form of two network producers who have heard my idea for doing a once-a-week, hour-long television series drama about a pro-football team, to be called either "The Team" or "The Coach."

"It's a real great idea, Rust," they say to me. "Out of *sight*." They are as convinced as I am that not only all those millions and millions of pro-football fans will watch the show, but so will all their wives and kiddies, because of the dramatic interest. *Everybody* will watch it, they feel; the other channels might as well suspend broadcasting in our time-slot. And with the kind of ratings we'll get, the network will have to let us do Real Good Serious Stuff. The coach is to be an angry, attractive man, like the old snarling Ben Casey; many of the shows are to be written so the plot can be resolved in action on the field. It'll be a real breakthrough, because there's never been a successful sports drama on TV before. I'm to act as producer and story editor, with a big budget and enough freedom to get important writers to do script ideas.

"Ted here and me," says one of the producers, "we'll handle all the business and technical stuff, make sure things go easy for you. The network says they can only give you seventy-five grand salary, but you'll get a share of the action, and when the reruns start, believe me we'll all clean up. The crew is all set to do the pilot as soon as we know whether Burton can get out of those commitments; Peck called again today, drooling for the role."

"Oh, I forgot to tell you," says Ted. "Swifty Lazaar keeps calling and calling. I think he wants to get in on this somehow."

I CUT PROUST

Or they come to me as Joe Fox and Jim Silberman, two old acquaintances who are now big and bigger at Random House.

"As you know, Rust," they say to me, "Proust's *Remembrance of Things Past* is only available in America (except for a few individual volumes in Modern Library) in that big, boxed, two-volume edition that Random has been selling like mad for years and years. There's more to publishing than just making money, though. We're worried that not everyone who buys the book, reads it. You have any ideas?"

"Well, Joe and Jim," I say confidently, "as *you* know, Edmund Wilson makes the distinction between Proust the philosopher and Proust the social novelist. Proust is much admired as a philosopher in France, but in England and America what we relish is his incomparable ability as a novelist. For many readers, unfortunately, Proust's story telling proceeds so slowly, clogged by his philosophizing, that they stop reading. I suggest an abridged Proust— wait, don't look so shocked, Joe and Jim, let me explain

—a shortened version of the whole book that would emphasize Proust-the-novelist. It would be a big book anyway, perhaps six or eight hundred pages. With a few transitional, explanatory paragraphs that we could insert in italics, the story would emerge luminously. Reading just *Swann's Way*, or only part of it, is actually a far more violent abridgement of the whole than is the condensed version I'd prepare. How alert of you to think of me to do this!"

"Listen, Rust," Joe and Jim say excitedly. "Your idea is exactly what we think we had in mind. Could you do it in a year? We'll give you a good royalty and a fat advance and help you get a grant from Rockefeller or Ford. We assume you'll want some travel money to go around and discuss the project with the leading Proust scholars. They'll be envious of you, of course, but they'll realize that a trained fiction editor is what's needed here and that as a long-winded writer yourself you'll just naturally know how to cut the daylights out of Proust. If you want, why don't you and your wife go live in Paris for the year you're working on it?"

I BENEFIT AMERICA IN TWO WAYS

Or, they come to me from the Treasury Department, having heard of my great idea how to supplement the federal government's revenue and benefit America at the same time. It's to put a one-percent tax on advertisements placed in all media: if advertising is, say, a three-hundred-billion-dollar industry, then the one-percent tax would produce three billion dollars each year, which would be turned over to education, just as the tax on gasoline is turned over to road-building. My tax would benefit America by discouraging advertising, which is bad, and by encouraging education, which is good.

One of the Treasury Department men looks very much like a man I had to spend three awful hours with discussing my income tax. "Everyone in Washington is very impressed," he says, in his distant, meticulous way, "that a man who self-admittedly hasn't much of a head for figures could come up with such a viable idea." It turns out that they want me to come down there and "head things up" for them until the plan gets started. "It would be a service to your country," they say, "and you might enjoy spending a year in Our Nation's Capital." Every time a letter arrives from the Internal Revenue Service, I think it will be about this, but it isn't.

MY CARIBBEAN YADDO

Sometimes in the early winter, when the sun's about to go down at three-thirty in the afternoon and the house is drafty from the north wind and there's no one around and everyone there is is boring, they come to me about what to do with this Caribbean island. A distinguished committee comes to me from Columbia University, comprised of Dean Barzun, Lionel Trilling, Robert Gorham Davis, and two or three trustees in banker's gray with very faint pinstripes. It seems that a millionaire has left Columbia a small Caribbean island with just the millionaire's mansion and a dozen or so guest bungalows on it. The university had considered selling it to add to the general endowment fund, but it seemed too ideal a place not to use in some way . . .

"Writers!" I say to them. "A place for writers!"

"You mean a writing school?" says Barzun, pursing his lips and looking at the others as if to say: Not a bad idea.

"Well, yes, that's part of it," I say, thinking fast. "A graduate school of writing, offering a Master of Fine Arts degree, run something like the famous Iowa Writers' Workshop, except it wouldn't be way out in cold Muddy River City Iowa, but on this neat hot island."

"But listen," I say to the committee, "if this island is all you say it is . . ." They nod to reassure me of the beauty of its beaches, its superb climate, the elegant accommodations. ". . . then it can benefit American literature in a far more significant way. What I have in mind, gentlemen, is a sort of writers' retreat, like The MacDowell Colony or Yaddo. It would be a sanctuary for our writers to create in, away from all the turmoil and boredom of their households."

I hear approving murmurs from the committee and notice them turning to smile congratulations to one another for having come to the right man with their island problem.

"All the major American writers would want to have a resident term there," I continue. "They wouldn't have to *teach* the students exactly, just expose themselves to the ones they were interested in. . . ."

"Mr. Hills!" warns Barzun, glancing at the trustees.

"You know what I mean," I say. "The thirty young, inexperienced, golden-tanned writing students would learn technique from the established older authors just by being in close proximity night and day."

"A Caribbean Yaddo . . ." I muse to myself, beginning

to daydream in the middle of my daydream. It seems to be the morning after a great debauch, and we're all lying on the beach recuperating. I overhear two golden students on a nearby beach-mat:

"That was a *marvelous* discussion last night, wasn't it?" says one girl.

"*I'll* say," answers the other. "But it's always real great when Saul and Norman and Vladimir get to arguing about techniques of point-of-view method with Rust. He's really smart, that guy."

"But *kindly*, too," says the first.

I AM THE COFFEE BASKET KING

No sooner had I gotten back from the Caribbean than they came to me from the Container Corporation of America—two executives and two lawyers, all with briefcases. They'd heard about my idea to sell coffee in small, sealed, airtight packages, the coffee contained in its own disposable percolator basket. The advantages are many: it is possible to have freshly opened coffee each time you have coffee, and not have what you don't use go stale in an opened can; the coffee is scientifically measured for your taste enjoyment, in two-, four-, six-, eight-, and ten-cup sizes, never too strong and never too weak; the disposable basket means you can throw the whole thing into the garbage can and not waste a lot of time rinsing out the basket and trying to flush the grounds down the kitchen drain.

"Oh, it's a selling idea all right, Mr. Hills," they say to me, "and it's very much in touch with the times. Nowadays people don't mind paying a bit more for a time-saving, labor-saving convenience like this. Frankly, we'll make millions from it: we've already got Alcoa, Reynolds, and Kaiser all bidding against one another. But our proposition to you is that you don't concern yourself further in it. You've had the idea: from now on it's just a matter of mass-marketing. We suggest that we buy the idea from you outright, and then we'll lease patents to the various coffee companies as consumer demand forces them to come to terms with us. We will pay you a hundred thousand dollars a year for the next fifty years— the money to be paid to your heirs, of course, in the case of your untimely demise. With this money you could do whatever you want: buy an estate on Fishers Island, for instance, and live out there quietly, working on your oil paintings, which we understand are *excellent*."

So then I daydream awhile about being out on Fishers Island—the du Ponts, the Lorillards, the Hillses, and the Rockefellers all together—me, "the Coffee Basket King," as the locals call me, working on my simple oil paintings—just monochrome water, a plain dark strip of land, flat dull sky—but museums vie for them.

I TELL BILL JOVANOVICH WHAT'S WRONG WITH AMERICAN PUBLISHING

Sometimes they come to me in the form of just one person: Simon Michael Bessie, director of Atheneum, on his way back from Martha's Vineyard; or William Jovanovich, head of Harcourt Brace, on his way from Rome or somewhere; or some impressive publishing person like that—at any rate, one man, and he wants to stop and see me here in Connecticut in the country, where we can talk quietly, away from the distractions of his hectic life.

He offers to take me out to lunch, but I decide we'd really have a better meal at home. At the table I made, looking out at the cove through the bow window I put in, we have a delicious cheese soufflé or chicken salad or something, and over a good bottle of light wine we get to talking about publishing. It's what he's come for: to hear what I have to say.

The trouble with publishing (I tell him) is the screwed-up relation between power and editorial ability. If a man is an able editor, he rapidly rises in a publishing organization and achieves power, yes—but as an executive editor or as an editor-in-chief, whose duties eventually become almost entirely managerial. His abilities as an editor are lost to the company: he no longer has the time to work carefully with authors on the preparation or revision of their work; he no longer can get out and around and find Promising Young Writers; he can no longer publish an individual book with the attentiveness and enthusiasm necessary to make it a success, to write the letters about it to key people, to give it the proper kind of publication party, to consult with the author about all his good ideas for boosting sales. *But* (I conclude), if you don't give this able young editor the power, then his ability to publish the book right will be thwarted by officious nitwits in advertising, sales, and administration, who know little about how books should be published, and certainly don't know the best way to publish any one particular book.

Jovanovich or Bessie or whoever it is sighs. He raises his wineglass and considers it in the afternoon sunlight coming through the coveside window, then sips it appreciatively. "Well . . . ," he begins, but then interrupts himself: "Those ducks are buffleheads, aren't they? Isn't it amusing how they dive down and bob up that way?"

I smile in agreement. In the winter, when the cove isn't frozen, I spend far more time watching the buffleheads than I care to admit to this busy man.

"Well," he says, "of course you are right in your analysis. But what suggestions would you have for remedying the situation?"

There is a pleasant pause while I consider my answer. The irony is (I say finally) that the best young editors don't really want the power, but feel they must have it to publish their books right. So don't give them power over other editors' books or for the list as a whole, but do give each and every editor control over how his own books are handled . . .

"By God, let's try it!" says Jovanovich or whoever. "Why don't you come in with us and publish just a few books a year? You'd determine the print figure, the ad budget, the design of the book and jacket, the promotion campaign, give a big party for each of your books. You'd even have control of sales distribution on each title. If you say, 'Three hundred and fifty books to the Hartford area,' then three hundred and fifty books to the Hartford area it is. You could live and work up here . . ."

"No," I say, gently restraining the mounting enthusiasm he feels for this plan. "No, you must give this power to each of your *young* editors, while they're still enthusiastic, not to a soured old veteran like me." I smile at him. "Your offer to me is of course very flattering, but I don't think I'd care to go back into publishing again. You know of course what Thoreau said in explanation of his leaving Walden Pond: 'Perhaps it seemed to me that I had several more lives to live, and could not spare any more time for that one.' No, I don't feel I could make as

122

substantial a contribution in publishing now as I could in some other area."

"Well," he says sadly, "publishing's loss will be mean a tremendous gain to some other field. You are one of the few people in America today who knows his own mind. Here's to your future—I know it will be brilliant." He drains his glass. "This wine is really superb. Would you be terribly affronted if I took the label and had Sherry-Lehmann send you up a half-dozen cases as a slight token of my appreciation for the time you've given me?"

Then he leaves, and I'm left just sitting here, still with nothing whatever to do—except look at the damn ducks. Also, I worry that he'll have some way of knowing how often I use that Thoreau quote. But then when I mull over things that he said—like "If you say three hundred and fifty books to the Hartford area, then three hundred and fifty books to the Hartford area it is"—then I know I've had a good daydream.

I AM APPROACHED
FOR THE BIGGEST JOB OF ALL

A day or two after Jovanovich's visit, Edmund Muskie, Hubert Humphrey, Eugene McCarthy, and Edward Kennedy arrived in a limousine. They'd come to plead with me. They were all stepping aside, forgoing their own ambitions—"for the sake of the nation," as they put it. They all wanted to help run my campaign as Democratic candidate for the Presidency of the United States. That's because they'd finally heard my great plan for How to Solve America.

How to Solve America

My solution to the problem of America came to me shortly after—and more or less as a result of—reading the newspaper on January 19, 1968, an historic date. It's not historic, even to me, because that's when I thought of my solution for America: I've told God's own amount of people about my plan, and while everyone agrees that it's a great plan, no one's implemented it yet; and obviously it's no good just having a plan, you've got to implement it, especially these days; otherwise you might just as well not have a plan at all. No, January 19, 1968, seems to me historic because surely the American low point was somewhere about that time: Lyndon Johnson was our President (which is a lot of low point just on its own); we were still escalating in Vietnam (toward our low point there, the Siege of Khesanh and the Tet Offensive, not much later); we'd had eighty-three straight months of economic growth (you'll see why that's bad in a minute); and there were all kinds of other things wrong. I keep thinking things have gotten somewhat better since, but I'd be hard put to explain exactly how. Maybe that's just because after I got the solution I became less interested in the problem.

At any rate, the newspaper I read that morning was the *New York Times,* and reading it started off like reading it every morning: so many ironies, so much to deplore. I remember how my grandfather used to rattle the paper in rage at FDR, but I am convinced that that was different: Roosevelt's policies threatened my grandfather's personal financial interests. The rage, the outrage I feel, stems from a similar sense of frustration—a sense that everything's being done wrong, and that I'm powerless to stop it—but it is different in that usually there's nothing in the newspaper that threatens my own personal financial interests. And maybe that's just because I don't actually have all that many personal financial interests.

Every once in a while, though, there is something that strikes, as the cliché goes, *close to home.* Reading the paper that morning, I was struck rather closer to home than usual by the opening passage of Eliot Fremont-Smith's review of an edition of the poems of the late Frank O'Hara:

> "Hell," cries the painter in Frank O'Hara's dramatic monologue, *Franz Kline Talking*—"Half the world wants to be like Thoreau at Walden worrying about the noise of traffic on the way to Boston; the other half use up their lives being part of that noise. I like the second half. Right?"

This indeed and quite literally struck me close to home. The place I care most for *is* my home—my house and outbuildings and twenty acres of land on a cove in Stonington, Connecticut, between New York and Boston.

It is also between New London and Providence, between Mystic and Westerly, Rhode Island, and between Route 1 and the big new Route 95. Route 95 is just barely too far away for us to hear, although one winter night when the cove was frozen over I walked out on the ice in the starry night and clearly heard the faint high whine of truck tires in the distance. Route 1 crosses a bridge perhaps a quarter-mile from the house, down-cove toward the mouth; and when the wind is fresh and from the north, we never hear the traffic on it either. But when the wind is from the southwest (and that is the prevailing wind), the sound of traffic can be clearly heard—if one listens. If one doesn't listen, one doesn't hear it, for the noise is not loud and there is much else to hear: birds, dogs barking, children calling, outboard engines, friends talking—for it is a busy place to say the least, a madhouse sometimes, people coming and going, arguing over croquet, trying to organize picnics, shouting as a horseshoe clangs onto the stake—all the noises of things one does at a country place.

Yet sometimes, I find myself alone there in the late fall or early spring. It is an important time for me. There are days that are cold and wet and foggy, when the sky seems low above, when the wind has dropped, and the birds and dogs and outboards are all still. I am perhaps working about the place, or maybe just walking around, looking at my land, my trees, my dock. Suddenly I look up, perceiving the extraordinary noise. Out of the mist, across the water, the water itself acting as a great sounding board, megaphoned up the cove from the road, comes the growl and whine and roar of traffic. It lets up, shifts, grinds, socks in again with a sort of a whoosh or thump as two trucks pass, lets up again, and I hear the sound gradually fade away, and then the growing wail of another car approaching in the distance. I put my hands over my ears. I love this place. It is what I have always wanted. Why do I let this noise bother me? It is not so bad, or it is only some days that it is bad. Yet each year it grows worse, as strip-development continues between Mystic and Westerly; and someday, I know, Route 1 must be widened to four lanes.

One half of the people in America, Frank O'Hara has Franz Kline say, are "worrying about the noise of traffic on the way to Boston." It is for me so literally the case that I have to make an effort to see how it can function as a symbol in his poem. Yet I know that it does, and it is a good one. It is a symbol of that one half of us who are the old, the fussy, the retired, the out-of-it, the complainers, withdrawn and frustrated and powerless, the constant deplorers. And there's "the other half who use up their lives being part of that noise," those who are busy and active and energetic, effective and perhaps powerful, doing things, getting things done, going places, getting somewhere, making it. O'Hara/Kline say that they like the second half: they want their art to be with-it, to be part of ongoing life.

For some reason I clipped the O'Hara review from the paper that morning and happened to turn it over. There on the back was James Reston's column, headed "Washington: 'Why, Then, This Restlessness?'" Reston was referring to something President Johnson had said in his State of the Union message to Congress two days earlier. Here is the passage of the speech in which it occurs:

> Now let me speak of some matters here at home.
> Tonight our nation is accomplishing more for its people

than has ever been accomplished before. Americans are prosperous as men have never been in recorded history.

Yet, there is in the land a certain restlessness, a questioning.

The total of our nation's annual production is now above $800 billion. For 83 months this nation has been on a steady, upward trend of growth. All about them, most American families can see the evidence of growing abundance.

Higher paychecks; humming factories; new cars moving down new highways; more and more families own their own homes equipped with more than 70 million television sets; a new college is founded every week. . . .

Why, why, then, this restlessness?

Because when a great ship cuts through the sea, the waters are always stirred and troubled.

And our ship is moving—and it's moving through troubled and new waters, and it's moving toward new and better shores. . . .

I remember seeing President Johnson give this speech on television. There was always something about the manner of that man when he was in the White House that drove me up the wall—my dislike of him was certainly as great and perhaps as irrational as my grandfather's dislike of Franklin Roosevelt. I grew cold with rage when I heard him talk about "new cars moving down new highways" and "more than 70 million television sets"—as if it were *good*, all this. "Who needs it?" I kept saying, "Who *needs* it?"

Can it be true that this nation is in fact divided between those who want more new cars moving down more new highways and those who think what we need is *fewer* cars moving down *fewer* new highways? Divided between those who love to be always zipping up to Boston to do whatever it is they do there, and those who sit by the side of the road hating the noise they make.

James Reston, in his analysis of the President's speech, makes the point that seems so obvious:

> This is a divided nation today not alone over economic but over fundamental moral questions. . . .
>
> We have come to see that prosperity is not, after all, the goal in the "pursuit of happiness," and that after all the boasts of 83 months of economic boom something is still wrong.

Even in prosperity we feel that something is wrong in America. That is, it seems to *some of us* that something is wrong. To those who are getting their first new car, their first TV—those who don't *have* twenty acres on a cove —it must seem a different matter. Can it be that this "fundamental moral" division in America is nothing more than the tedious, traditional, bitter old one between the haves and the have-nots? Who needs it indeed? Who needs it is who hasn't got it.

We are coming now to what I believe is called the crux of the matter. Here it is, *the crux:* We've already got too many cars, say—let's take just cars, because they strike so close to home. Yet there are still a lot of people who don't have cars, and they want them. You can't keep them from having cars if they want them. How would you like not having a car? But if we get many more new cars going down many more new highways, our country-side will soon be all turnpike-and-parking-lot. This is simple-minded, I know, but it is the crux of the matter: continued economic growth, more "progress," and more "abundance" are going to make this country not worth living in.

My solution for the problem of America resolves this paradox, takes into account all the psychological-sociological aspirations of the citizenry, and as well cures all our economic ills. In fact, my idea for how to solve America could solve the rest of the world as well.

That's because the rest of the world still sees our problem as its solution. In that same newspaper there was a series of stories on Japan's fantastic rate of economic development. This is the sort of thing no normal man would ever dream of reading, but being struck close to home isn't very pleasant, especially in the morning when one is having his coffee and reading his paper, and it tends to make one read the rest of the news more sensitively:

> TOKYO.—According to economic analysts, every Japanese aspires to own the "Three C's"—color television, car, and cooler (air conditioner).
>
> In too many cases, economic prosperity has been gained at the cost of certain individual sacrifices, and developments in one field have caused disruption in another. Critics note a deterioration in family and neighborhood relations as the pursuit of material comforts assumes greater importance.

This Tokyo story came from a special supplement in the paper, "The *New York Times* Economic Survey of Asia and the Pacific." Every country mentioned in it appeared to have made the same commitment: to some insane conception of "progress" as an end, to achieve economic "growth," as if growth were something that could ever be achieved. Every underdeveloped country wants to become a modern industrial power like the United States or

Japan. Isn't there one country somewhere that can see that what's paid for the color TV, the cars, the "coolers," is never worth it? Not only not worth it, but that the cars and TVs aren't advantages anyway, but disadvantages? And that air conditioners aren't necessary if you don't pollute the air with factories making them? Hasn't this all happened enough times and enough places already for anyone anywhere to have learned anything? Is it all going to go on and on until the whole world looks like Queens Boulevard?

HONG KONG.—One of the most picturesque aspects of Hong Kong is coming to an end. The boat people are gradually coming ashore. . . .

For more than a century of Hong Kong's existence as a British colony the boat people have been one of its colorful human spectacles.

Until they began to move ashore some years ago there were 100,000 to 150,000 who passed all their lives aboard craft clustered in vast, bobbing fleets of wooden hulls, soaring masts and reefed sails at a half dozen main sheltering sites.

Cheerful illiterates, the boat people sing and laugh, dress in tattered garments, wear jade bracelets for luck and set off firecrackers to scare away evil spirits. . . . Children start helping with boat chores as soon as they can walk. . . .

Years ago the Hong Kong government began to encourage the boat people to move ashore. . . . Huge blocks of small apartments have been built for them and about 45,000 have been lured to life on land.

"It's like dragging cave-men out of the forest," said a resettlement officer. "They are bewildered by a kitchen and haven't the slightest idea what a toilet is. It takes them years to accommodate to apartment living."

Why should they want "to accommodate to apartment living"? I lived in an apartment a good deal of my life and I sure as hell don't see anything so great about it. Living on a boat is much better: wealthy industrialists spend millions on yachts and never have the time to use them. I suppose it's humiliating to be part of "a colorful human spectacle," rafted up as a tourist attraction; yet look at the quai-side in Cannes and you'll see rich people doing it for pleasure. "Children start helping with boat chores as soon as they can walk." Why is it better to get them ashore in an apartment to watch color TV?

Why? Why? Why? That's the whine of the man who deplores the noise of the traffic on the way to Boston, and it's no more pleasant than the whine of the traffic itself. Why the Vietnam quagmire? Why the space race? Why a new lousy college every week? Why drag "cavemen out of the forest"? Why drag these happy underdeveloped countries into the wretched modern world? Why ruin their countryside, their waterways, the very air they breathe?

Clearly America leads the way in all this, like a Judas goat; clearly all the other countries follow, like little lemmings determined to get their share of the future. Yet Americans are manifestly more nervous and insecure and restless—less happy—than the "simple" people of these "underdeveloped" nations. Even President Johnson noticed this. He said it was because when our great ship of state is on the way to better shores, the boat's bound to make waves. But some of us, up to our necks in this crap, mumble the punch line of the famous joke: "Don't make waves." And anyway, we're *not* on our way to better shores; we're on our way to *worse* shores; we may even be headed straight out to *sea*. That's what makes some of us who sit by the side of the road want to get off the boat. We are all dismayed by the quality of our life. There's nothing wrong with the quantity, I guess; unless, as I say, there's too much of it. The country as a whole—the countryside and the cities, the look of America—is getting uglier and uglier. Mrs. Johnson's beautification campaign did just what we expected it would: nothing. Each reader can fill in the specific things he specially deplores about modern America; but the point, again, is that everything is getting worse instead of better. Everyone knows this, but let me give some examples so that you deplorers can nod in agreement and cluck your tongues.

When a building is torn down in New York City or anywhere in America, the building that is put up instead is, with some very few exceptions, uglier and worse built. Even the brownstone tenements are better buildings, solider and better-looking than the slum-clearance architecture which replaces them. The old rambling farm buildings are better than the flimsy development houses. Factory architecture in this country has gone from solid old stone buildings, beautifully windowed, through red brick, to tinny aluminium sheds with fluorescent lights. It is now too expensive, or something, to put up good buildings. Older buildings are almost always better— houses, apartments, factories, whatever. Everyone knows this.

What is true of buildings is pretty much true of everything. *Boats:* The old wooden sailing yachts with their lovely lines were infinitely better than the awful molded-plastic, humpbacked modern ones. *Roads:* The beautiful old winding country lanes were incredibly much better than the snarling new superhighways; they were lovelier and made less noise, and that's better. *Ham:* Old-fashioned cured or hickory-smoked or whatever-it-was ham was much better than the artificially flavored and tenderized supermarket kind—and that's true of almost all foods. *Pots and pans:* The old-fashioned heavy iron or copper ones are much better than the lightweight new ones—ask the cooking experts. *Fences:* Who wouldn't prefer a lovely old stone wall or a white picket fence to the monstrous heavy-chicken-wire or cement-block modern ones? And what is true of buildings, boats, roads, hams, pots and pans, and fences is true of virtually *anything you can name:* always the old was substantially, demonstrably better than the new.

Everything was better before. Rivers were unpolluted and beautiful. The air was better—smelled better, looked better, *was* better. There are only a few remote areas left free of the sounds of automobiles, and none where you can't hear airplanes. Large cities are nightmares of noise and soot and strikes and riots; small cities are getting that way. The small towns are finished, the farmland and woodlands between them being turned into parking lots for giant shopping centers and drive-in movies. It all looks and sounds and *is* awful. Everyone knows this, and aside from a few advertising space salesmen and real estate developers, everyone admits and deplores it.

In sum, the quality of life in American today is so speeded up, so complex, so ridden with choices of no real difference, so fluid and unsupportive in social structure, so *mass*-everything, that our people are confused, anxious, lost, lonely, and nervous—in a word, not-very-happy.

We've got too many things, and most of them are ugly and shoddy and unnecessary, and anyway they're always breaking. We can't keep them in order. We can't order our lives. Sociologists tell us of the anomie; psychologists tell us of the neuroses. No one can ever actually be made happy by the way things are going, with all this growth and progress, everything growing worse and progressing in what's clearly the wrong direction.

The problem of America, then, is one hell of a problem.

But, fortunately, my solution is also one hell of a solution.

So what am I going to do about it? How are we going to solve America? You can't slow down or stop all this growth and progress without causing disaster to the economy; we know that. My solution for America takes this into account. It takes *everything* into account.

How to solve America is profoundly and beautifully simple: *just turn everything around and start going the other way.* This would keep America moving, but now we'd be moving in the right direction, backward—from the complex back toward the simple, from the new back to the old, from the ugly and shoddy back to the lovely and the sturdy.

The idea, basically, is to decide today to undo tomorrow what was done yesterday, day-after-tomorrow undo what was done day-before-yesterday, and so on—with some important variations and refinements—backward in time, until we get just the kind of America we used to have and liked so much.

This would cause no unemployment, because there'd be just as much work undoing all the things we've done recently as there was doing them; actually it will be *more* work, the way we're going to do it. The real cause of unemployment is mechanization, right? Well, not only are we going to demechanize America, we are going to demechanize her, in so far as possible, quietly and slowly, without using any noisy machines, and that's going to be a lot of work. No de-assembly lines: men will take computers apart using just screwdrivers and pliers. So actually this job of painstakingly dismantling modern America would require fantastic amounts of manpower —and rebuilding the old America would take even more, for we'd have to relearn the skills and attitudes of good workmanship. For instance, the tunnels under the rivers around Manhattan would have to be undug, and the bridges unbuilt—both dangerous and time-consuming jobs. Then the ferry boats that the tunnels once replaced would now have to be rebuilt to replace them—and because wood is going to be at a premium in this new, older society, until we can get some trees to grow again —the ferries would have to be built of available scrapwood by skilled shipwrights. Taking down skyscrapers will be done carefully, too—with no noise or dust. Hardhats will stand proudly and respectfully and quietly as the mayor says a few grateful words to them at the joyous ceremonies celebrating the unlaying of a cornerstone. Taking up the asphalt and concrete would be done by friendly groups of overweight businessmen working easily together with sledgehammers and crowbars, for the sound of the air compressor and the jackhammer would pass from the land. And as the good earth is revealed again under all the crud we've put over it, how lovely it will be! Perhaps a tenth of our men and a quarter of our women will have to work as landscapists and gardeners for a while—not just as a hobby, as they do now, but as their work. Imagine finding pleasure in work!

There would be a great need for people to raise and train horses. What a job it would be to dismantle all the automobiles, melting down all the steel and ultimately replacing it in the ground in a form as close to iron ore as possible. Everything—steel, concrete, plastics—all would go back into the earth where it came from. What planning it would require to get it all put back neatly into place! Archivists would search the records to determine what existed previously in each area; long-range planners would speculate about what existed even earlier; and implementers would plan older, slower ways to achieve it.

The intention wouldn't be to take the nation as a whole back to an aboriginal state, living in caves and tepees and hunting from ponies, or anything like that—although that style of life would be available for those who wanted it. What's to be achieved is a return to some sort of approximation of the American ideal, having the best of each era, without anybody being exploited.

Thus, most Americans would live in small towns, but there would be isolated rural areas and there would be moderate-sized, tenable, livable cities for those that wanted them. The economy would be basically agricultural—small farms, unmechanized, family-owned, and family-worked—but there would also be small, local industries manufacturing things *well*. There would be traveling companies of repertory players, putting on plays in renovated movie houses of each village. Books would be published in each city, sold in the bookstore in each town. Everything would be much cheaper, the way it was before we got mass-production. Saturday afternoons there would be baseball games, and one would play—or watch men one knew play—against the teams of other towns. People would once again know where they belonged, who they were.

We would take something of the best from each era, but very little of the very modern would endure. There could, for instance, be a few quiet old-fashioned airplanes, kept as museum pieces for those that wanted them; but no jetports, nothing remotely resembling a jetport. There would be old, grand, luxurious trans-Atlantic liners and romantic tramp steamers, as well as lots of sailboats, not just yachts, but fast clipper ships and working schooners. An adequate train service might remain, or be re-created —with elegant dining cars, as in days gone by. All the elevated highways and the throughways and the parking lots would be replaced with trees and grass, of course; but there might be a few hundred cars left, for the nuts. That disturbing nuisance, the telephone, would go, as soon as we didn't need it. Electric alarm clocks would go right away—in fact, alarm clocks won't be necessary, for people will go to bed early, sleep well in the quiet, and arise refreshed, the way they once did. All the noisy inconvenient "conveniences" of modern life will disappear more or less in reverse order of their appearance— the snowmobile taking precedence over all others, however, no matter what newer horrors they've thought of by the time we start this.

The family will assume a vital role again, as demechanization creates chores inside and outside the house for older people and for children. In coastal areas children may be able to help with boat chores as soon as they can walk. "Community" will come to mean something good again, too, as the process of urbanization is reversed.

There'll be a need to subvert and eventually obvert our national mania that "growth" is a good, that it is "vital." A nation that is really vital, we can say, is one that endures in its best phrases, that refuses to grow toward its own extinction. We must make our Gross National Product *less* gross, more refined. Those in charge of our bureaus of government must show a substantial decrease in all aspects of their organizations at year's end, or be replaced by can-undo men who will. Advertising men must devise campaigns that imply that owning a car will make you feel, not young and sexy and rebellious as now, but old, worn out, and subservient. Eventually advertising will disappear, too, except for useful announcements of events and services and perhaps a few of those nice old Burma Shave signs by the side of the road. Conglomerates need to be unconglomerated; mutual funds need to be unmutualized; everything *mass*-must be made as individual as possible as soon as possible.

Those who have difficulty dismantling their own modern appliances can pay others to do it for them, earning money themselves in some kind of demerchandising, like arranging for the giant chain stores in the shopping centers to be divided up into village general stores, or starting old-fashioned bakeries with delicious nutritious fresh-baked bread, or local butcher shops with tender local beef placidly raised cropping some local hillside into a lovely meadow instead of being toughened by being whooped at and "git along"-ed at up and down some trail out West and then packed and processed in Chicago. But by and large, men and women would want to do as much of their own work as they could. Independence would once again become a virtue, which is good, and also become possible, which is even better. With despecialization, demechanization, and a general decomplication of everything, then ingenuity and resourcefulness and real know-how would gradually again become part of the Yankee character. And gradually, too, as more and more of the complexity had been removed and buried and grown over, Americans would once again be faced with work that they could handle and understand, that had real meaning for them, that told them something about themselves.

When America, the leading industrial power in the world, thus rejects industrialism, we can be sure that the Germans and Japanese, great emulators of The American Way, will reject industrialism too. Emerging nations will stop emerging, take a second look, and go right back into the forest. In fact, it won't be many years before America will feel a real rapprochement with the other underdeveloped countries of the world. And when they start sending us teams of advisers, think what that will do for world peace.

Doesn't it all sound nice? An ease and a peace will come over the restless, troubled people of this land, as gradually out of the noise and grime and busyness of our "civilization" appear once again the rolling plains and the farms and the wooded hillsides.

Isn't this a good plan for how to solve America? It is only necessary now to implement the plan. I know you're anxious to get started, but I don't really recommend your doing it on an individual basis. I mean, if you and I, say, and our families, started undoing tomorrow whatever it was we did yesterday, and so on back the way the plan has it, but just all by ourselves, we're not going to have any effect on the traffic on Route 1 or on anything else for that matter; we'll just end up further behind than usual, in a tremendous financial and social mess—as long as everyone else is still going the regulation way. No, the plan has to be implemented collectively, and the best way to persuade people to do something collectively is to pass a law saying they have to. I suggest that on the federal, state, and local levels, all legislatures pass a law with the same wording, to show we're all behind it, and the executive departments of government agree, and the courts declare it legal in advance, and all the media support it and promote it and explain it and analyze it, the way they do, so that everybody's clear about it: that we're going to turn America around and start going the other way.

How would it be paid for? How, I ask you, was all this mess built in the first place? People were somehow sold on the idea that they wanted all these junky new things. Already we find many Americans seeking just the opposite: *paying* to go on a boat ride around Manhattan, even if the boat doesn't take them anywhere, the way the old ferries did; *paying* to have a cottage way out in the country somewhere; *paying* to go on camping trips —and the more primitive the conditions, the more they pay. Do you know what it *costs* to ride in one of those horse-drawn carriages through Central Park, or to ride and keep a horse anywhere? The whole country—even Chicago—is ready for it. It would be twice as easy to persuade Americans to get rid of all this junk as it was to persuade them that they wanted it in the first place. In fact, once a kind of conspicuous *de*consumption pattern started, it would be hard to control. Who would want to be last on his block to get rid of his color television set?

A Final Note

Anyone of a theoretical-analytical bent of mind with time on his hands (the only kind of person who would have finished this book) is bound to find some of the enjoyment I do in reading around in a book published by the Philosophical Library (New York) called *Dictionary of World Literature: Criticism, Forms, Technique,* edited by Joseph T. Shipley "with the collaboration of 250 Scholars and Other Authorities." What a first-rate way to spend time this book is! For instance, the *E*'s—really, the *E*'s may be the best part of the book. The *E*'s begin marvelously, with *ecbasis,* listing some of the forms of rhetorical digression. If the digression is simple, it is called *Diexodos.* If it is "by lengthy divagation," it is *Parecbasis.* If it is "by turning back to try another tack," it is *Anachoresis.* If it is "in order to explain," it is *Exegesis* ("still in general use"). There are, of course, other forms of digression listed, and the note adds that "All may be found in *Tristram Shandy*"—that wonderful, long-winded book. I keep meaning to go back to *Tristram Shandy* and track down the examples of all the forms of digression, but there just doesn't seem to be *time* these days to do worthwhile things like that.

There are all sorts of fine things in the *E*'s. William K. Wimsatt puts his initials on a little explanation of "elegant variation," the fault of style that occurs when you go out of your way not to repeat a word. There are longish summaries of "English Criticism" and "English Versification" and "Epic Poetry" and then a piece on the "Essay," which is why I brought this all up in the first place.

The "Essay" essay is initialed "H.G.M." and one deduces from the list of "Advisers and Contributors" in the front of the book that this is Harold G. Merriam of Montana State University. He begins by saying that "What the essay is has never been precisely determined," but "in general, it is a composition, usually in prose, of moderate length and on a restricted topic." Not much to quarrel with there. But then he strings all the kinds of essays out on a scale (diagramed) that runs from those characterized by "Formality" (on the left) to those characterized by "Informality" (on the right). "At the extreme left," he says, "such writings as treatises and monographs will place themselves." Then he has in the middle "editorials," "book reviews," "magazine and newspaper articles," in that order. Then: "After the midmark to the right will appear 'characters,' impressionistic writings, personal essays, playful essays, sketches."

I keep puzzling over this diagram every time I can grab a spare moment—once every two years at least. I *like* diagrams. But this one seems pretty feeble to me, and there's a lot about the whole arrangement that doesn't seem right. In college I thought a lot about drama forms, and since then as an editor I've been involved with novels and especially short stories, and I've thought a lot about the forms of them; but I've never thought much about the essay. It doesn't seem to me, though, that by-degree-of-informality can be the best way to divide the essay form up into kinds and sorts. I often wish Wimsatt had done this piece: he's a whiz at categorizing things. There must be a better way than this, but even if there isn't, has Mr. Merriam got it right, even by his own system? Is the "Editorial," for instance, really more formal than the "Book Review"? But much more important than that, from my point of view at least—and this is *really* why I brought it all up—is the question of whether the "Treatise-Monograph" and the "Personal-Playful Sketch" are inevitably at *opposite* extremes of the essay form. What I tried to do in my essays was combine the two, and I hadn't any intention of doing anything *extreme*. But Mr. Merriam goes on to remind one that it was Montaigne who first used the word *Essais* when he published his "confessional comments" in 1580, and that the word means "attempts." Without (God knows!) trying to liken oneself to Montaigne, I suppose one may *attempt* anything.

LRH